More
Disputed Questions
in the Liturgy

John M. Huels

Liturgy Training Publications

This book was edited by Martin F. Connell.
Deborah Bogaert was the production editor, and
Theresa Houston provided additional editorial
assistance. The layout is by Jill Smith. The book
was typeset by production artist Mark Hollopeter
in Times.

Printed in the United States of America.

Library of Congress
Cataloging-in-Publication Data
Huels, John M.
    More disputed questions in the liturgy/John M.
Huels.
        p. cm.
    Includes bibliographical references and indexes.
    1. Canon law. 2. Catholic Church — Liturgy.
I. Title.
LAW
264'.02 — dc20   96-46520
                                                    CIP

ISBN 1-56854-171-6
MOREDQ

Contents

Abbreviations **vi**

Introduction **1**

Unauthorized Liturgical Adaptations:
   Inculturation or Abuse? **9**

Preparation for the Sacraments:
   Faith, Rights, Law **33**

The Sunday Mass Obligation **61**

Daily Mass: Law and Spirituality **73**

The Liturgy of the Hours in Parishes **85**

Penance: Individual or Communal? **97**

Sacramental Sharing with Other Christians **113**

Reception of Sacraments
   by Divorced and Remarried Persons **129**

Eucharistic Reservation **153**

The Age for Confirmation **167**

Lay Preaching at Liturgy **179**

Acknowledgments **193**

Index of Canons **195**

Index of Liturgical Laws **199**

Abbreviations

AAS	*Acta Apostolicae Sedis*
BCL	Bishops' Committee on the Liturgy (United States)
CCEC	*Code of Canons of the Eastern Churches*
CDF	Congregation for the Doctrine of the Faith
CLD	*Canon Law Digest.* Edited by T. Lincoln Bouscaren and James I. O'Connor. Vols. 1–6, Milwaukee/New York: Bruce, 1934–1969. Vols. 7–10, Chicago: Canon Law Digest, 1975–1986. Vol. 11, Washington: CLSA, 1991.
CLSA	Canon Law Society of America, Washington, D.C.
DOL	*Documents on the Liturgy 1963–1979: Conciliar, Papal and Curial Texts.* Collegeville: Liturgical Press, 1982.
GILH	General Instruction of the the Liturgy of the Hours
GIRM	General Instruction of the Roman Missal
HCW	Rite of Holy Communion and Worship of the Eucharistic Mystery Outside Mass
ICEL	International Commission on English in the Liturgy
LTP	Liturgy Training Publications, Chicago
NCCB	National Conference of Catholic Bishops, United States
NDSW	*The New Dictionary of Sacramental Worship.* Edited by Peter E. Fink. Collegeville: Liturgical Press, 1990.
OICA	*Ordo Initiationis Christianae Adultorum* (Latin typical edition of the RCIA, 1972)
RBC	Rite of Baptism of Children
RC	Rite of Confirmation
RCIA	Rite of Christian Initiation of Adults, U.S. version (1988)
RLI	Instruction on the Roman Liturgy and Inculturation
SC	Vatican II, Constitution on the Sacred Liturgy, *Sacrosanctum Concilium*
UR	Vatican II, Decree on Ecumenism, *Unitatis redintegratio*
USCC	United States Catholic Conference

Introduction

This second volume of
"disputed questions" was prepared by invitation of Liturgy
Training Publications following the initial success and
steady demand for the original volume, *Disputed Questions
in the Liturgy Today,* published in 1988. In that book
I addressed the following: the age for confirmation, lay
preaching, female altar servers, concelebration, Mass
intentions, reducing the number of Masses, first confession,
general absolution, who may be anointed, mixed marriages
and the eucharist, and concerts in churches. This new
volume treats eleven other issues.

**1. Unauthorized liturgical adaptations: inculturation
or abuse?** Priests, deacons and others sometimes make
changes in the rites that are not authorized by liturgical law.
Canon law says that no one may change anything in the
liturgy on their own authority. Yet Vatican II is widely

understood as having called for the liturgy to be adapted to the culture and mentality of the people. So are all unauthorized liturgical adaptations "abuses," or are some of them appropriate ways of inculturating the liturgy? How does one tell the difference between a good adaptation and an abuse?

2. Preparation for the sacraments: faith, rights, law. Do non-practicing Catholics have the same rights to the sacraments for themselves and for their children as do practicing Catholics? Can Catholics who are otherwise eligible to receive a sacrament be denied a sacrament because they cannot or do not want to participate in a sacramental preparation program? What is the relationship between personal faith and the suitable disposition required for receiving the sacraments? The answers to these questions often vary from pastor to pastor and from catechist to catechist. This chapter provides authoritative answers to these disputed questions based on canon law.

3. The Sunday Mass obligation. The law requiring participation in the eucharist on Sundays and holy days still exists. This law, which was very strongly upheld in previous generations, is rarely so emphatically taught anymore. This essay looks at the historical antecedents of the law and the approach to it by canonists and moralists both before and after Vatican II. It then addresses the question of whether a greater emphasis on the Sunday obligation in catechesis and in preaching might help reverse the decline in attendance at the Sunday eucharist, or whether a different approach would be more effective today.

4. Daily Mass: law and spirituality. Some liturgists believe that the routine celebration of daily eucharist in parishes should be eliminated. But there are members of the faithful, notably clergy, religious, seminarians and some lay liturgical ministers, who are obliged to attend Mass every day in virtue of particular laws or job expectations; and there are laity who willingly attend every day. This essay looks at three distinct "spiritualities" of daily Mass that are implied in canon law and offers suggestions on how each of these three spiritualities might be harmonized to make daily eucharist a better experience for all who choose — or are obliged — to participate in it.

5. The Liturgy of the Hours in parishes. A disputed issue
that surfaces from time to time is whether Liturgy of the Hours
rather than eucharist is the more appropriate form of daily
liturgical prayer. Although the celebration of one or more daily
Masses is common in most parishes, the celebration of the
Liturgy of the Hours is not. This chapter offers pastoral
suggestions to assist parish leaders in introducing this important
form of liturgical prayer and celebrating it regularly. It then
relates this parish challenge to the contemporary understanding
of the clerical obligation to recite the Liturgy of the Hours daily.

6. Penance: individual or communal? The Roman Ritual
provides an individual rite and communal rites of penance.
Popular participation in the individual rite has dropped dramatically since Vatican II, whereas large crowds come for communal
penance. Yet church law is exceedingly restrictive on the
possibility of using the rite of general confession and absolution.
Does that mean communal penance should be abandoned in
favor of individual confession? This chapter explains the
canonical issues involved and gives pastoral suggestions so that
communal celebrations of penance can be celebrated lawfully
and effectively.

7. Sacramental sharing with other Christians. Can the unity
of the church be fostered when Christians of various churches
take part in and receive the eucharist in each others' churches, or
must sharing in eucharistic communion be possible only after
ecclesial union is achieved? This and related questions are
addressed in this chapter. It is an updated and revised version of
an essay originally published in my 1986 book, *One Table, Many
Laws,* which is out of print. It was updated principally in view
of new provisions in the 1993 *Directory for the Application of
Principles and Norms on Ecumenism.* Although there are
significant canonical restrictions on sacramental sharing,
a proper interpretation of the law reveals that there are greater
opportunities for sacramental sharing than many people realize.

8. Reception of sacraments by divorced and remarried persons. This essay addresses some of the issues surrounding the traditional church teaching that persons who are divorced and remarried, or those who have married a divorced person, are to be excluded from the sacraments. In particular, it looks at whether they can be admitted to the sacraments by means of the so-called internal forum solution, as three German bishops have taught, or whether the pope and the Congregation for the Doctrine of the Faith have altogether forbidden the use of this pastoral solution. In some respects this is more a matter of moral theology than an issue of liturgy and canon law. However, with about 40 to 50 percent of marriages ending in divorce, the issue has a major impact on the ordering of the eucharistic assembly.

9. Eucharistic reservation. Questions and conflicting views about the reservation of the eucharist arise frequently today. This occurs especially when churches are being built or renovated, or when small groups or individuals want to reserve the eucharist solely for the purpose of adoration. This chapter shows that church law offers clear answers to these questions.

The final two chapters revise and update issues treated in the first volume of *Disputed Questions*. There have been legal developments regarding both since 1988, and both remain hotly disputed pastoral issues.

10. The age for confirmation. This issue will not soon be resolved, at least not in North America. In Canada there is no fixed age for confirmation, except for the age determined in approved catechetical programs, which theoretically could include ages lower than seven. In the United States, it is possible for each diocese to establish a standard age within the range of seven to eighteen years. In light of this flexibility, it is incumbent that parents, catechists, pastoral ministers and *confirmandi* be aware of the theological and liturgical values at stake in this debate, as well as the canonical issues, such as the right of a qualified seven-year-old to receive the sacrament.

11. Lay preaching at liturgy. This topic is developed at greater length in this volume than in the previous one, addressing not only the legal issues but also the liturgical and pastoral values behind the law. As the number of qualified lay ministers continues to grow, the question of whether a lay person may preach at liturgy arises with increasing frequency. The issue that is most disputed is whether lay persons may preach at the eucharistic liturgy.

A few words should also be said about some significant legal developments that affect several of the issues I treated in the original *Disputed Questions*. On the issue of female altar servers, my essay gave the legal arguments for and against altar servers and concluded that it was lawful for women and girls to serve at the eucharist. I had first stated this position in an article I had written for *Worship* in November 1983, at the time the revised code went into effect. The position I took was subsequently adopted in 1992 by the Pontifical Council for the Interpretation of Legislative Texts and made public in 1994.[1]

Another legal development occurred on the issue of Mass offerings and intentions. This essay in the 1988 book addressed problems and pastoral solutions associated with the practice at the eucharist of announcing and praying for special intentions for which a monetary offering was given to the priest. In 1991 the Congregation for the Clergy issued a decree that permits the practice of taking more than one offering for a single Mass, observing the rules established by the decree.[2] With the possibility of several, perhaps many, special intentions at the same Mass, there is still the need to be aware of the concerns addressed in that essay.

On the issue of general absolution, the Holy See did not approve the 1988 "interpretation" adopted by the National Conference of Catholic Bishops of the United States that defined as "one month" the "long time" *(diu)* that individuals would have to be deprived of sacramental grace or holy communion before they could receive a general absolution. The reason given was that the Holy See did not consider it a decree needing approval.[3] Since the *recognitio* of the Holy See was necessary for legal force, the U.S. "interpretation" is not binding but has more the character of a guideline. Diocesan bishops remain free to establish their own diocesan policy on general absolution and are not bound to accept the NCCB's interpretation of the meaning of *diu.*

In my earlier volume I concluded in the essay on mixed marriages and the eucharist that marriages involving a Catholic and a Protestant generally should not occur at a eucharistic celebration, in part because of the symbolic distortion that occurs as a result of the Protestant guests being unable to receive holy communion. The 1993 *Directory for the Application of Principles and Norms on Ecumenism* admits the possibility that a Protestant party may receive communion at the wedding Mass, as I had argued, but this does not affect the other Protestant guests who may not be invited to communion.

Another notable development in canon law since the 1988 volume was published was the promulgation in 1990 of the first code for the Eastern Catholic churches, the *Code of Canons of the Eastern Churches* (CCEC). The Latin church and the various Eastern Catholic churches have their own liturgical disciplines, so most of the issues treated in this volume are not likely to be of great interest to Eastern Catholics. However, church laws and teachings on divorce and remarriage and on ecumenism are largely common to all the Catholic churches, so relevant canons from the Eastern code are also cited in the chapters on these two topics.

NOTES

[1] AAS 86 (1994): 541; *BCL Newsletter* 30 (April 1994): 13.

[2] AAS 83 (1991): 443 – 46; *BCL Newsletter* 27 (1991): 13 –16.

[3] *The Jurist* 53 (1993): 404.

Unauthorized Liturgical Adaptations: Inculturation or Abuse?

Anyone who has gone to different churches for the eucharist will have noticed not only that there are different styles of celebration (music, preaching, presiding) but also that sometimes certain parts of the Mass are changed in some way, chiefly by omitting or adding something or by using words different from those in the lectionary or sacramentary. The reaction to these differences can be positive or negative. Visitors are heard to say "I wish we had Mass like this in our parish!" Or they say the opposite: "I'm sure glad I don't have to worship here every Sunday!" The good experiences are no accident: They are the result of parish ministers and an assembly who truly care for their liturgy and know how to celebrate it well. The poor celebrations are those where, on the one hand, apathy and a minimalistic approach to the liturgy prevail, or, on the other hand, where well-intentioned people make bad choices because they lack solid formation in liturgy.

Often the poorly celebrated liturgies violate no liturgical laws. For example, where the sign of peace is never exchanged or communion from the cup is never given, no law is broken; but the faithful are deprived of powerful signs of their communion in Christ with God, with one another and with all the baptized. This kind of liturgical neglect, while a serious concern, is not the issue here. Rather, only innovations that are contrary to liturgical law are considered — both good and bad adaptations.[1] One could argue, of course, that anything contrary to law is an abuse. Yet it is not uncommon to find that some unauthorized adaptations actually make the liturgy a better experience, more prayerful, more vibrant, more meaningful and more fully expressive of the rite being celebrated.[2] Should such intentional changes be relegated to the same level as abuses due to negligence, ignorance, casualness or convenience?

One cannot look to canon law for authorization to make changes in the liturgy at the level of the individual minister or the liturgy committee. In fact, canon 846, §1, which is based on the *Constitution on the Sacred Liturgy,* 22, §3, says the opposite: No one may add, remove or change anything in the liturgy on their own authority. However, Vatican II also taught that "even in the liturgy the church does not wish to impose a rigid uniformity in matters that do not affect the faith or the good of the whole community"; ministers "must, therefore, realize that, when the liturgy is celebrated, something more is required than the mere observance of the laws governing valid and lawful celebration."[3] Canonists and specialists in liturgical law have long recognized that the prohibition in the law against making changes in the liturgy is not absolute, that it must be harmonized with the overall principles of the liturgical reform, especially the goal of full, conscious and active participation by all the faithful.[4] No serious scholar has argued for a return to the rubrical absolutism of the pre-Vatican II church.

Canon 846, §1 is a forceful statement of the necessity to observe the rites of the Roman liturgy in their integrity, but it should not be interpreted apart from the spirit of the *Constitution on the Sacred Liturgy.*[5] The law certainly means that changes in the liturgy that substantially alter a rite cannot be admitted at the local level. Such major adaptations are possible only by the conference of bishops in accord with the norm of law (SC, 40, 63 – 69). However, minor adaptations that help make the rites more meaningful and expressive of their true nature are generally welcomed or at least tolerated by church authorities. Most bishops appear to have no difficulty with such adaptation when it serves a good purpose. A familiar example is the priest's invitation to the assembly before the prayer over the gifts using the adapted words "Pray, brothers and sisters" rather than the words of the text, "Pray, brethren." The pastoral benefit of this adaptation is obvious to anyone familiar with the contemporary concern that all forms of communication be inclusive of both men and women when both are intended.

The diocesan bishop is the principal authority for the oversight and regulation of the liturgy in his diocese (canons 381; 391; 392; 835, §1; 838, §4). He has authority over the public exercise of the liturgy by all, including members of pontifical religious institutes (canon 678, §1). He can enact liturgical laws, provided they are not contrary to universal laws (canon 135, §2). He can grant dispensations from universal law, including dispensations from universal liturgical laws (canon 87). The universal law entrusts to the bishop authority to decide whether it is appropriate to use certain approved rites or practices, such as general absolution (canon 961, §2) and eucharistic processions (canon 944). He also regulates non-liturgical prayers and devotions (canon 839, §2).[6]

With the bishop's broad canonical powers over the regulation, promotion and custody of the liturgy, it is he who can judge authoritatively whether an innovation in the liturgy is an abuse to be eradicated or a practice that may be tacitly accepted due to its value for the liturgy and thus for the church. Of course, the bishop does not have the power to prevent a practice approved by universal law, nor can he impose a practice contrary to universal law. Recourse against a bishop's decision of this nature could be taken to the Holy See. The prudent bishop also bears in mind the long-standing maxim in the canonical tradition adopted from Roman jurisprudence: *de minimis non curat praetor,* or, the praetor (or high-ranking official) should not be concerned

11

with minor matters. The oversight of liturgical details is best delegated to the diocesan liturgical director or the diocesan liturgical commission, except when the bishop's direct intervention is needed to eradicate abuses. Ideally, the bishop's intervention should not be necessary. With proper formation, every liturgical minister should be able to judge the difference between a good adaptation and a bad one.

The title of this chapter frames the question in terms of "inculturation" versus "abuse." Sometimes "inculturation" is considered a matter pertaining to new churches in mission territories where the indigenous culture has relatively recently come into contact with Christianity. However, there is another sense in which inculturation applies to all local churches everywhere. In this sense of the word, every church must find the best way to celebrate the liturgy according to the culture (or cultures) of its people. This does not mean that any adaptation in the liturgy done in the name of the people's culture is a good adaptation. In 1994, the Congregation for Divine Worship and the Discipline of the Sacraments issued an instruction on the inculturation of the Roman liturgy which established the principles that must be observed in correctly adapting the liturgy.[7] Although this instruction is intended chiefly to address the adaptations made by episcopal conferences, many of the principles it contains are equally useful for judging the suitability of local adaptions.

The first part of this essay sets forth and explains select principles from canon law, the *Constitution on the Sacred Liturgy* (*Sacrosanctum Concilium,* SC) of Vatican II and the *Instruction on the Roman Liturgy and Inculturation* (RLI). These principles are fundamental for making correct judgments about the propriety or impropriety of a liturgical adaptation at the local level. In the second section, some of these principles will be applied in three cases of adaptations contrary to liturgical law that have been introduced in some places in North America and elsewhere.

I. Principles

1. Ecclesiastical laws are to be understood according to the proper meaning of the words considered in their text and context (canon 17). Before it is possible to judge whether a new or different practice in the liturgy is a good adaptation or an abuse, it is necessary to know the pertinent liturgical law. One must first determine how the innovation in question relates to the laws of the liturgical books, the *Code of Canon Law* or other sources of law, such as the decrees of the conference of bishops or the diocesan bishops. After the relevant laws are identified, the process of interpretation begins. Liturgical laws are part of the body of church law, called canon law, and they are interpreted according to the same rules as other kinds of ecclesiastical laws. Canon 17 gives a key rule of canonical interpretation: One must look at the text and the context of the law. The text of the law is situated in an immediate context along with other laws as a section of the liturgical book or document of which it is a part. The context situates the law among other laws in the section treating the same issue, and reading these other laws helps one to understand what this particular law means.

The context is not just the other laws connected with the one under consideration, however; it also includes other information that may shed light on the law's meaning, especially the historical and theological contexts. What is the history of the law? How was the matter treated in the past? Why did the law evolve this way? Knowing the law's history gives the interpreter a greater ability to make a more nuanced judgment about any particular adaptation of the liturgy. The theological context of ecclesiastical laws is also important because canon law is a theological discipline, albeit practical rather than theoretical. Behind church laws there often is some theological teaching or concept being expressed in a practical norm. The interpreter of liturgical law who has a foundation in sacramental and liturgical theology will be a better interpreter of liturgical law than the person who lacks it. That is why liturgists frequently are more adept at interpreting liturgical law than are canonists.

In promulgating the *Code of Canon Law* in 1983, Pope John Paul II said that the code must be interpreted in light of the teachings of Vatican II.[8] This is a standard principle of canonical interpretation today. Canon law must be interpreted in light of the council, not the council in light of canon law. For the interpretation of liturgical law, the *Constitution on the Sacred Liturgy* of Vatican II has paramount importance, although it is not an exclusive referent because in some cases the liturgical reforms have progressed beyond what was envisioned in 1963 when the constitution was promulgated. Thus, the various postconciliar liturgical documents from the Holy See may also be important sources of contextual information for understanding any given law regulating the liturgy.

2. In the church, the salvation of souls *(salus animarum)* **is the supreme law (canon 1752).** Canon law exists to assist the church in its salvific mission. Law is in the service of the church, not the other way around. Church laws are truly at the service of the church only when they are upholding some value, some good, that in some way, even remotely, assists the church in its mission. In fact, behind every church law there is some value being implied, and the good interpreter seeks to identify what that value is. It may be discovered that the value the law seeks to uphold was a response to a historically conditioned situation that no longer exists today; or it may be a value applicable in some cultures and not in others; or it may be a theological opinion disputed by Catholics; or it may be a truth of the faith that is universal for all times and for all cultures. Such an inquiry may suggest that the value behind the law is obsolete, that it does not apply in this culture, that it does apply in general but not under these particular circumstances or that it is essential and can never be changed or neglected. It is not possible to make these kinds of judgments unless one has first done the work of discovering what value the law is intended to uphold.

3. All the faithful should receive instruction on the liturgy. More intensive liturgical formation is necessary for liturgical ministers, in accord with their function and roles (SC, 14 – 20). Without liturgical formation, it is not possible to reach good judgments about liturgical practices, to understand the values expressed in liturgical laws, to know the difference between a good adaptation and an abuse or between a variation that serves to promote the spirit and nature of the rites and one that detracts from them. Many variations observed in the liturgy are not genuine adaptations but are merely mistakes resulting from ignorance, carelessness, minimalism or bad taste. No innovation should be attempted by anyone who has not had solid liturgical formation. Even priests, who have significant theological and pastoral preparation, may not be capable of making adaptations that conform to the nature and spirit of the liturgy. They are best advised to keep to the rubrics and the official texts, which, after all, were prepared by experts.

The principle is simple: The more one knows about liturgy, the more readily one can distinguish a good adaptation from an abuse. The practice is more difficult, because liturgical expertise does not come without serious effort, both through initial coursework and through ongoing study.

4. Full, conscious, and active participation in liturgical celebrations by all the faithful is demanded by the very nature of the liturgy (SC, 14). This well-known principle was the cornerstone of post – Vatican II liturgical reform. It is also a key criterion for assessing whether an adaptation is acceptable or not. Does the adaptation lead the faithful to fuller participation in the mysteries? In answering this question, one should keep in mind that there are various kinds of active participation: singing and praying aloud, gesture and movement, prayer in silence and active listening to the word of God proclaimed and preached. It is also possible, at appropriate moments in a liturgy, that an assembly is actively involved emotionally, spiritually and aesthetically in listening to a choral work or an instrumental piece or watching liturgical dance.[9]

5. In liturgical celebrations everyone should carry out all and only those parts which belong to their role or ministry (SC, 28). Active participation does not mean that everyone must say and do everything in the liturgy. The liturgy is "hierarchic"; it is ordered according to distinct roles and ministries. The presider does not proclaim all the readings, play the organ and take up the collection. The deacon, lay ministers and assembly do not say the prayers of the presiding priest (canon 907).

6. Liturgical services are not private functions but are celebrations of the church; they pertain to the whole church, manifest it and have effects upon it (sc, 26; canon 837).

Liturgical celebrations are communal in nature, not individual. Communal celebration is the norm; individual celebration, even of the Liturgy of the Hours, is the exception to the norm. The celebration of the liturgy in the parish is not the private preserve of any group, even of the parishioners themselves. All the faithful have a right to enter any parish church for the liturgy (canon 1214), and it follows that they have a right to find there the Catholic liturgy, not a liturgy so different from elsewhere that they feel alienated. The parish liturgy must be one that welcomes and accommodates the stranger, the marginalized, those of different classes and cultures, and those with differing levels of faith and commitment.

A strong tendency in contemporary North American culture is to evaluate the meaningfulness of social interactions on the basis of their ability to create experiences of intimacy, closeness, bonding and interpersonal sharing; this value often transfers to people's expectations of the liturgy.[10] Certainly in small, homogeneous groups, such as on a spiritual retreat or in Marriage Encounter or Cursillo, the participants often experience a particular emotional closeness to one another at the liturgy due to the special experiences they have shared; but these situations are temporary. Parish liturgy cannot re-create these intense experiences, nor should it try. The parish is not a homogeneous group of like-minded intimates and friends. The parish is a microcosm of the church, and its liturgy is the public liturgy of the church.

The parish liturgy is the public worship of God, not a surrogate for group therapy. Consequently, the parish liturgy ought not be adapted to such an extent that only the in-group feels a part of it. Rather, it should seek to offer sacred time and sacred space for all the baptized to worship together and experience their true unity as members of Christ's body. (See RLI, 22 and note 82.)

7. Inculturation responds to the needs of a particular culture and leads to adaptations which remain faithful to the substantial unity of the Roman rite (SC, 38; RLI, 36). There must be no innovations unless the good of the church genuinely and certainly requires them, and care must be taken that new forms adopted should in some way grow organically from forms already existing (SC, 23; RLI, 46). Like all ritual, the Roman liturgy has a standard, normative structure that is regularly repeated by the participants, who at each gathering enact afresh the familiar patterns. This substantial unity of the Roman rite must always be preserved when adaptations are made. The liturgies of each of the sacraments require, for validity, certain essential elements (such as bread and wine) and certain words (the sacramental forms). No one may alter these essential requirements other than the supreme authority of the church — the pope or an ecumenical council (canon 841). Otherwise the sacrament is invalid. This rule also applies to the substitution of inclusive language for masculine titles of God and Christ in the sacramental formulas, such as Father and Son in the formulas of baptism and penance.

In addition, there are essential ritual structures that, while not required for validity, pertain to the authentic nature of a rite, for example, the liturgy of the word and the liturgy of the eucharist in the Mass. In both the liturgy of the word and the liturgy of the eucharist, there are in turn certain parts that may not be omitted, even if their content changes, for example, the presidential prayers, the scripture readings and the eucharistic prayers. Adaptations in the liturgy may not alter or omit its essential structure and basic parts.

Innovations in the liturgy should not be introduced merely for the sake of novelty but only when they are genuinely and certainly for the good of the church. The good of the church is twofold: both the good of this particular assembly, which may require or recommend that there be some adaptations, and the good of the church universal, which expresses its unity, catholicity and orthodoxy through a common worship that is faithful to the substantial unity of the Roman rite.

8. The rites should be distinguished by a noble simplicity. They should be comprehensible to the people, but there should not be a need for numerous explanations for them to be understood (SC, 34; RLI, 35). The liturgy communicates religious meaning not only through texts and words that are read, prayed and sung, but also through signs, actions and art forms. These symbolic forms convey meaning at a deep, pre-conceptual level; they directly touch the "soul" (emotions, memory, the unconscious). When the liturgy is done well, when its fundamental signs are not obscured but are expressed in their fullness, then there is no need for any explanations or commentaries during the liturgy itself. Explanations reduce the power of symbol by detracting from the immediacy of the experience. The intellect's craving for explanations should be satisfied through formation apart from the liturgy, such as through mystagogia, the post-liturgical catechesis that deepens one's understanding and appreciation of the mysteries already experienced.

9. The liturgy is not a performance; music, dance movements and gesture must always be the expression of true communal prayer of adoration, praise, offering and supplication (RLI, 42). The *Instruction on the Roman Liturgy and Inculturation,* in saying the liturgy is not a performance, means that it is not a form of entertainment whereby certain "performers" (the ministers) put on a show while the audience passively listens and watches. At liturgy, all the participants perform the rite; all are to have an active part in the celebration in accord with their proper role.

The communal worship of God should engage the whole human person, body and spirit, intellect and emotions, but this engagement must be appropriate for liturgical prayer. Not all elements of a culture are suitable for liturgical adaptation. The liturgy, if it is to be true to the gospel, must often be counter-cultural. In a culture that is formed to a significant extent by television, there are inevitably going to be conscious or unconscious expectations that the assembly (the "audience") must be entertained in novel ways, as is their regular habit in front of the television. In this environment it is a counter-cultural statement for believers to gather, not passively to be entertained but actively to give praise and thanks to the divine creator because it is truly right and just to do so.

Because everyone in a television culture is susceptible to treating the liturgy as entertainment, it is important that the assembly's leaders, especially the presider and leader of song, establish a proper tone and adopt a style suitable for the worship of God. Their attitude, their manner of speech and their way of singing and praying sets the example for others. It sometimes appears that the television talk show or variety show is the model adopted by ministers at the Sunday eucharist. They begin with a cheery "good morning," introduce the other "performers," tell a joke and continue the "show" in their role of chatty host or star performer. Their casualness with liturgical speech and symbol betrays their unease with religious ritual and their lack of conviction in its inherent power; they are more comfortable as entertainers, especially in the role of the star of the show where the spotlight is on them. The style they adopt and the adaptations they make in the liturgy point to their own cleverness or amiability; such adaptations lead to the cult of personality, not the cult of God.

The tendency to adopt an entertainment model at liturgy is not limited to liturgical musicians and presiders but includes deacons, readers and all who have a ministerial role. It also applies to the assembly itself, whose experience and expectations of gathering in social groups has largely been that of "audience" looking to be entertained. Could this be the reason for the popularity of periodic novelties that surface at the Sunday eucharist, like children's pageants, clowns and polka bands?

10. The church approves of all forms of true art which have the requisite qualities and admits them into divine worship (sc, 112). Music, architecture, the visual arts (statues, paintings, mosaics, stained glass) and the design of vestments, furnishings and liturgical objects have long been vehicles for the inculturation of the liturgy. New questions are arising today as musicians and other artists, together with liturgists, attempt new ways to inculturate the liturgy through the arts. Some liturgical musicians have composed sung acclamations for the eucharistic prayers in addition to those approved (the Sanctus, Memorial Acclamation, Amen, and the acclamations of the children's eucharistic prayers). Is this appropriate adaptation? What about background music during the recitation of the eucharistic prayer? Is liturgical dance permissible at any point in the liturgy? May there be dramatic readings of the gospel involving several readers rather than just the deacon, concelebrant or presider?

Questions about the liturgical arts and inculturation are difficult to treat in the abstract because art is not an abstraction. One cannot assess a song without seeing the text and hearing the music. One cannot assess the value of a liturgical dance until it is danced.[11] These are aesthetic and ritual decisions, matters of good taste, good liturgy and sound pastoral judgment. They also raise the question of the talents and abilities present in a community. A religious choral work by a great composer might, in the abstract, be an excellent work of art, but if the parish choir cannot sing it well, it does not belong in that particular liturgy. The art form must also be ritually appropriate. A choral anthem could well be suitable during the collection or as a meditation after communion, but it cannot replace the responsorial psalm or another part of the liturgy in which the assembly should be singing. The same is true with musical settings of the eucharistic prayer, dramatic readings, liturgical dance and other innovative art forms. They must be good art, performed well, and be of service to the community in its worship of God.

When a church is built or renovated, canon law requires that experts knowledgeable in liturgy and the sacred arts be consulted (canon 1216). The same should be true when other art forms are incorporated into the liturgy. Not every pastor or liturgy committee can be expected to have knowledge of the liturgical arts; not all have good taste. Liturgical musicians and other liturgical artists should have a sound education in their art as well as adequate liturgical formation. When they are competent in their ministry, the other liturgical planners will have greater confidence in their suggestions for inculturating the liturgy through their art.

10. The first significant measure of inculturation is the translation of liturgical books into the language of the people (RLI, 53). The universal adoption of vernacular languages in the liturgy in place of Latin has been one of the most successful aspects of liturgical reform and, perhaps more than anything else, has served to promote full, conscious and active participation by all the faithful. It is still permissible to celebrate the liturgy in Latin provided the reformed rites are used (canon 928), but this would be contrary to the principle of active participation if the assembly does not understand the Latin language and is not capable of singing or responding.

This is not to say there is no role for Latin in the liturgy. The church desires that its treasury of sacred music, especially Gregorian chant, be preserved.[12] Anyone who has participated in a papal audience in Saint Peter's Square and sung the Our Father in Latin with tens of thousands of fellow Catholics can readily recognize the value of a common linguistic tradition. Nearly everyone is capable of learning simple Gregorian chant settings, such as for the Sanctus and Agnus Dei. Their occasional use during the vernacular liturgy not only helps preserve a common cultural heritage but also is a cogent witness of the assembly's catholicity and its connection to other local churches in time and space.

A major issue in reference to liturgical language is the need for scriptural and liturgical texts to be perceived by everyone as inclusive. In another publication I treated this subject from a canonical perspective in some detail, showing that English-speaking bishops' conferences favor the use of language that does not exclude women where both men and women are intended.[13] Since 1975, all translations of the International Commission on English in the Liturgy have observed this principle of inclusivity. Where the translations of texts before 1975 have not yet been revised or published, careful preparation before the liturgy is necessary so that any changes made for inclusivity are in conformity with the intent of the original text and are grammatically correct.

II. Cases

In this section, in order to determine whether they are good adaptations or abuses, some of the principles described above are brought to bear on three adapations of the liturgy that are contrary to liturgical laws. The adaptations are: (1) standing in place of kneeling during the eucharistic prayer; (2) reciting a Hail Mary at the conclusion of the general intercessions; and (3) washing women's as well as men's feet at the Mass of the Lord's Supper on Holy Thursday.

Standing During the Eucharistic Prayer

Gestures and bodily postures in the liturgy, which should "express the attitude of humanity before God," may be adapted in different ways according to the dictates of culture (RLI, 41). In English-speaking North America, the posture prescribed by the bishops' conferences during the eucharistic prayer is kneeling from the end of the Sanctus through the Amen. However, in some parishes and in many religious communities and seminaries, the assembly stands throughout the eucharistic prayer. Is this an acceptable variation or an abuse of the law?

Knowing the historical context of a law often sheds light on the law's interpretation. History reveals that the church has known standing for the better part of its history, especially at solemn Masses.[14] Kneeling was more likely to be known at the low Mass. However, in North America the practice was to kneel even at solemn high Masses. The 1969 *General Instruction of the Roman Missal,* 21 prescribed the posture of standing for the eucharistic prayer, with kneeling or genuflection at the consecration. (The word *genuflectant* has either meaning.) However, the GIRM allowed the conferences of bishops to adapt this posture, to change it to something else. In 1969 the United States bishops voted to retain the custom of kneeling. Their reasoning was political: Because this was a time of rapid and major changes in the liturgy, they feared that people would not absorb any more liturgical changes. The English-speaking Canadian bishops voted for the same adaptation. The bishops of Belgium, the Netherlands, France and Quebec opted for standing throughout the eucharistic prayer. In Spain and Italy, the bishops accepted the universal norm — standing throughout except for the consecration.

As noted above, a standard principle in the science of canon law today is that church laws must be interpreted in light of the teachings of Vatican II. For the interpretation of liturgical law, the *Constitution on the Sacred Liturgy* has paramount importance. A major emphasis of the constitution is that the liturgical reforms are to encourage and enhance the full, conscious and active participation of the people in all the liturgical rites.

Because posture is a means of participation, what the optimal posture is for the assembly's active participation during the eucharistic prayer needs to be asked. Ritually, standing is the posture that most befits active participation. That is why the presider and deacon stand throughout the prayer; they are clearly active participants. Kneeling is fitting for personal prayer and is associated with the veneration of the reserved sacrament. However, in the eucharistic meal and sacrifice, Christ is actively present; the eucharistic prayer is not a time for personal adoration of the reserved sacrament but for participation in a communal action, in the church's great prayer of praise and thanksgiving. This is not to say that there can be no participation by the people when they kneel but suggests rather that the posture of standing better signifies their baptismal dignity and better fosters a sense of their own active role in worship; they are not just passive spectators of an action going on at the altar.

Enough has been said to conclude that standing is no abuse of the law; in fact, it serves better the value of active participation than does kneeling. Although the U.S. bishops did not make the "ideal" decision in 1969 on posture during the eucharistic prayer, they voted for what they perceived was realistically the best solution at the time. In doing so, they believed that it was desirable to avoid burdening the people with too many liturgical reforms all at once. Their reason is one that should always be considered in adapting the liturgy. The Christian people should not have liturgical changes suddenly and arbitrarily foisted upon them without catechesis at the whim of the pastor or director of liturgy. For example, to force the assembly to stand by removing all the kneelers in church, as has occurred in more than one parish, meets with resistance and hostility, not with understanding and acceptance. The latter can only be achieved by thorough catechesis, by taking all the time that is necessary to explain a change and build consensus for it.

Hail Mary at the General Intercessions

It has been reported that, in a few places, the priest concludes the general intercessions by kneeling before the statue of the blessed virgin Mary and reciting the Hail Mary together with the congregation. Is this an example of legitimate inculturation?

On the one hand, it could be argued that it is a legitimate variation. The church, from the early centuries, has honored the mother of God in the liturgy and in popular piety, and devotion to Mary is highly commended. The intercessory role of the saints is a tenet of the Catholic faith; asking Mary and the other saints to intercede with God has long been a trait of Catholic spiritual practice. Marian piety is especially strong in the popular religion of certain cultures, for example, among Hispanics. Communal recitation of the Hail Mary may stir deep spiritual feelings in some people. Moreover, the Hail Mary is an approved prayer of the church and is highly regarded by the magisterium. The words of the first half of the prayer are from Luke's gospel; the second half of the prayer goes back to the early centuries of Christian devotion.[15]

On the other hand, there are weighty and convincing reasons against concluding the general intercessions at Mass with a Hail Mary. In the model general intercessions given in the sacramentary, the rubric states that the priest says the concluding prayer. The proper posture for all is standing. The prayer is always addressed to God, and it concludes by invoking the intercession of Christ. Mary surely has a place in the liturgy: She is remembered in the eucharistic prayers; many feasts are celebrated in her honor throughout the liturgical year; there is a special Missal, the *Collection of Masses of the Blessed Virgin Mary*, which has 46 Mass texts and accompanying scripture readings to be used for votive Masses throughout the year, especially on Saturdays. However, in none of these official texts of the Mass are prayers addressed to Mary. Prayers are addressed to God the Father and conclude through the intercession of Christ the Lord. Some liturgical prayers, such as the intercessions at the Liturgy of the Hours, are sometimes addressed to Christ, but no official liturgical prayers are addressed to Mary and the other saints.

Mary's role in the liturgy is principally that of model of discipleship for all Christians to emulate. This point is developed extensively in Pope Paul VI's apostolic exhortation *Marialis cultus*.[16] As the church recalls in the liturgy Mary's part in the mystery of salvation and her close connection to the saving events in the life of her son, it holds up Mary as an exemplar of what the Christian life is meant to be.

The *Constitution on the Sacred Liturgy,* 13 highly recommends sound expressions of popular piety but adds that, "by its nature, [the liturgy] is superior to them." The 1994 *Instruction on the Roman Liturgy and Inculturation* categorially states: "The introduction of devotional practices into liturgical celebrations under the pretext of inculturation cannot be allowed." In *Marialis cultus,* 48, Pope Paul VI praises the merits of the rosary but adds that "it is a mistake to recite the rosary during the celebration of the liturgy, though unfortunately this practice still persists here and there." What the pope said of the rosary applies equally to the Hail Mary, which is the basic prayer of the rosary: It does not belong in the liturgy. This is true of other devotional practices as well, such as the crowning of the statue of Mary with a wreath of flowers. However, there is nothing to prevent the recitation of the rosary or an annual crowning before or after the eucharist. This is akin to what is known as "acculturation": a popular devotion is juxtaposed with the official liturgy without being integrated into it.[17]

Washing Women's Feet

A rubric of the *Roman Missal* for Holy Thursday says that men are to be chosen for the rite of washing of feet. However, in North America it is common for both men and women to be chosen. At the time the Missal was published in English in 1970, the word "men" was still understood in an inclusive sense to mean both men and women. Few persons had access to the Latin original, where the male term *viri* was used, not the inclusive *homines*. Thus, the custom may have begun inadvertently in many places but took root after repeated use year after year. In 1988, the Congregation for Divine Worship issued a circular letter on preparing and celebrating the paschal feasts.[18] In paragraph 51, the circular letter states: "The washing of the feet of chosen men which, according to tradition, is performed on this day, represents the service and charity of Christ, who came 'not to be served, but to serve.' This tradition should be maintained, and its proper significance explained."

A few bishops in the United States used the pretext of this circular letter to insist that only men be chosen for the washing of feet. Actually, this letter was saying nothing new; it was merely referring to the Missal. In saying "this tradition should be maintained," the congregation was not so much emphasizing that it was the masculine nature of the feet that needed to be maintained but the tradition of the washing of feet itself, because it represents the service and charity of Christ. The washing of feet also recalls Christian baptism (John 13:2–10).[19]

On what basis may one judge whether the custom of washing the feet of both women and men is an acceptable variation or is an abuse of the liturgy? One important principle for good interpretation of law is to search for the values behind the law. Laws are based on some value, some good, that is being fostered or protected by the law. The best interpretation of the law is one that correctly understands the value and applies it within the context at hand, including the cultural context.

The liturgical laws governing the washing of feet seek to uphold the purpose and meaning of the rite; that is the value of the law. The purpose of the footwashing is the ritualizing of Christ's action and his command to do likewise — that just as he has come to serve, so must his followers be of service to the church and the world. The footwashing rite also refers to baptism and is thus a reminder to all in the assembly of the connection between their baptism and a life of discipleship. Thus the core theological value behind the liturgical laws governing the footwashing is the virtue of charity and the command to serve. This core value applies equally to males and females. All Christians are called to lead lives of charity and service; all have the right and duty to be disciples in virtue of their baptism (canons 204, 216). For Catholic people in many places, the washing of the feet of both women and men (and children) represents the common baptismal vocation of all.[20]

Church laws that are universal in scope must be applied with some flexibility according to the cultural dictates of a region and its peoples. In certain cultures, the washing of a woman's feet by a man in public would be a breach of etiquette or even scandalous. In those countries, it would not be proper to defy the local culture by imposing a practice that the people would find alien and offensive. In those societies, the universal law specifiying the washing of men's feet causes no difficulties. However, in North America, Europe and numerous other parts of the world, sensitivity to the equality and rights of women is a sign of the times, a fact of contemporary life. This fact cannot be neglected when the universal law is applied in such cultures. A literal application of a law that is perceived to be sexist is likely to be opposed or ignored, even if the law's observance is demanded by the bishop. Moreover, the equality of all the baptized is a principle enshrined in the fundamental, constitutional law of the church (canon 208). This principle is based on the divine law, to which merely ecclesiastical (human) law must defer. When a human law is perceived within a society as violating the principle of the equality of the sexes, it is not a good law in that context; it no longer is in the service of the church there. It is then necessary to correct the law in that local church by an appropriate remedy, such as dispensation or the development of a contrary custom (canons 85, 24).

Inculturation or Abuse? Additional Examples

Liturgical theologian M. Francis Mannion has observed: "The practical difficulties of carrying out appropriate adaptation of rites, both in Western and non-Western countries, have proved to be considerable. Theoretical agreement on principles does not translate easily into practical consensus."[21] Few people are likely to disagree with the principles enunciated in the first section above; but when these principles are put into practice, other criteria — such as personal taste or piety, one's own views on the role of liturgy, or cultural values and influences — can greatly influence how these principles are put into practice.

All of the following practices have been observed at liturgies in North America.[22] All of them are deviations from liturgical law and are either directly contrary to the law or simply not mentioned as options. Based on the principles above, which of the following could be appropriate adaptations? Which are abuses?[23]

1. The eucharistic ministers (and sometimes the priest) receive communion after the rest of the assembly.

2. The rites are ordered somewhat differently without omitting anything. For example, at a Sunday eucharist at which there is an infant baptism, the Mass begins with the welcome and initial questions of the baptismal rite; at a wedding, the Mass begins with the questions of intent from the wedding rite; the readings of the Easter Vigil are done before the lighting of the new fire; the sign of peace is given after the general intercessions.

3. The Profession of Faith is omitted on a Sunday.

4. A Christmas vigil Mass begins at 3:00; the Easter Vigil begins before dark.

5. The assembly is invited to approach the font to sign themselves with water in place of the rite of sprinkling.

6. Baptized candidates are included in the scrutiny rites; uncatechized Catholics are dismissed from the eucharist along with catechumens.

7. Customs like the unity candle, a lasso, or coins are used in the rite of marriage.

8. The presider uses colloquial greetings, such as "Good Morning!" or "Have a good day!"

9. The bread and wine are placed directly on the altar by "table setters" rather than handed to the ministers.

10. The paten and chalice are handed from person to person at communion, or the cup is taken from the altar rather than given by a minister.

11. Dancers or other ministers assist the presider at the sprinkling rite, doing some of the sprinkling themselves.

12. Feast days of Mary or of patron saints are celebrated on Sundays of Advent or Lent or on other days when this is prohibited.

13. Instead of choosing a focus for the liturgy based on the readings, other themes are chosen for the Sunday eucharist (pro-life, Mothers' Day, environmental awareness, etc.).

14. The presider or deacon uses words other than those prescribed in the liturgical books.

15. Gestures are omitted, such as bows and genuflections by the priest, the bow by all during the Creed, the signing by all at the gospel, the kissing of the gospel book, the striking of the breast by all during the Confiteor.

16. The priest displays the host at the elevation after the consecration in a sweeping movement from side to side, as at benediction.

17. The large host is broken by the priest during the institution narrative of the eucharistic prayer.

18. The gospel is proclaimed and preached from the midst of the assembly.

19. The hands of all present are washed on Holy Thursday instead of the feet of twelve persons chosen for this role.

20. Bread is consecrated only for the priest; everyone else receives the reserved eucharist from the tabernacle.

21. A deacon or lay minister presides on Good Friday.

22. An expanded version of a reading is given so that women are included, for example, Mary Magdalene on Easter Sunday (John 20:11–18 in addition to 1–9).

23. The eucharistic prayer includes short acclamations sung by the people in addition to those approved, as in the children's eucharistic prayers.

24. The organist plays softly during the recitation of the eucharistic prayer.

25. A lengthy gospel is divided into parts for a dramatic reading by several readers rather than just the deacon or priest.

NOTES

[1]The terms used by canonists and liturgists for such changes in the liturgy are chiefly "accommodation," "adaptation" and "inculturation." In 1986 Gerald A. Arbuckle forcefully argued that "adaptation" should be replaced by "inculturation." See "Inculturation Not Adaptation: Time to Change Terminology," *Worship* 60 (1986): 511–20. A few think that "accommodation" is the correct term for a variation introduced by the minister. Yet the term "adaptation" persists due to its general suitability to a variety of meanings. See Mark Francis, "Adaptation, Liturgical," NDSW, 14–25. On page 14, Francis defines liturgical adaptation as "the process by which the liturgy is modified in such a way as to render it 'more suitable,' 'more appropriate,' 'more meaningful' to a given group of worshipers in a given context." He points out that "the documents of the Second Vatican Council and the revised liturgical books use this word in a variety of contexts to express a range of nuanced ideas: from the most superficial kinds of rubrical changes to the creation of new liturgical forms springing from the genius of a particular culture."

See also Anscar J. Chupungco, "A Definition of Liturgical Inculturation," *Ecclesia Orans* 5 (1988): 11–23.

[2]See, for example, the description of an adapted rite for the preparation of gifts in Gabe Huck, "Many Other Things," *Liturgy 90* 24 (July, 1993) 14–15, and 25 (January, 1994): 14–15.

[3]SC, 37, 11. Translations from SC are taken from *The Liturgy Documents,* 3rd ed. (Chicago: Liturgy Training Publications, 1991).

[4]Among the canonists, see Walter J. Kelly, "The Authority of Liturgical Laws," *The Jurist* 28 (1968): 397–424; Frederick R. McManus, "Liturgical Law and Difficult Cases," *Worship* 48 (1974): 347–66; *idem,* "The Church at Prayer: Going Beyond Rubrics to the Heart of the Church's Worship," *The Jurist* 53 (1993): 263–83; Robert M. Garrity, "The Limits of Personal Accommodation in Sacramental Celebration," *The Jurist* 53 (1993): 284–300; R. Kevin Seasoltz, *New Liturgy, New Laws* (Collegeville: Liturgical Press, 1980); John Huels, "The Interpretation of Liturgical Law," *Worship* 55 (1981): 218–37. See also liturgist Thomas Richstatter, *Liturgical Law Today: New Style, New Spirit* (Chicago: Franciscan Herald, 1977).

[5]For further treatment of the proper interpretation of canon 846, §1, including its historical and theological contexts, see my essay "Liturgy, Inclusive Language, and Canon Law," in *Living No Longer for Ourselves: Liturgy and Justice in the Nineties,* ed. Kathleen Hughes and Mark R. Francis (Collegeville: Liturgical Press, 1991): 138–52.

[6]This latter competence is given to all local ordinaries, including the vicar general and episcopal vicar.

[7]The Roman Liturgy and Inculturation, Fourth Instruction for the Right Application of the Conciliar Constitution on the Liturgy, January 25, 1994, AAS 87 (1995): 288–314. Translation published by the Vatican, 1994.

[8]Cf. John Paul II, apostolic constitution *Sacrae disciplinae leges,* AAS 75 (1973), part II, xiii.

[9]See Congregation of Sacred Rites, Instruction on Music in the Liturgy, *Musicam sacram,* 15, March 5, 1967, AAS 59 (1967): 300–20. See also SC, 112 which says that

the church approves and admits into the liturgy all true forms of art that have the requisite qualities.

[10]M. Francis Mannion, "Liturgy and the Present Crisis of Culture," *Worship* 62 (1988): 98–122; Richard R. Gaillardetz, "North American Culture and the Liturgical Life of the Church," *Worship* 68 (1994): 403–16.

[11]Thomas A. Krosnicki has some thoughtful reflections on the role of dance in the liturgy. See "Dance Within the Liturgical Act," *Worship* 61 (1987): 349–57.

[12]SC, 114, 116; *Musicam sacram,* 47–53.

[13]Cited above in note 5.

[14]See John K. Leonard and Nathan D. Mitchell, *The Postures of the Assembly During the Eucharistic Prayer* (Chicago: Liturgy Training Publications, 1994).

[15]NCCB, pastoral letter, *Behold Your Mother: Woman of Faith,* 96 (Washington: USCC, 1973).

[16]Apostolic exhortation *On the Right Ordering and Development of Devotion to the Blessed Virgin Mary,* 4, 16-23, February 2, 1974, AAS 66 (1974): 113–68.

[17]Ansgar Chupungco describes an example of a Filipino Marian procession before the Mass at Easter dawn, approved in 1971 by the Congregation for Divine Worship, as an example of acculturation. See *Liturgical Inculturation: Sacramentals, Religiosity, and Catechesis* (Collegeville: Liturgical Press, 1992): 27–28.

[18]*Paschalis sollemnitatis,* January 16, 1988, *Notitiae* 24 (1988): 81–107; *Origins* 17 (1988): 677–87.

[19]See Martin F. Connell, "Except for the Feet: Initiation by Footwashing," *Liturgy 90* 27 (February/March, 1996): 4–7.

[20]The secretariat of the BCL issued a statement acknowledging the acceptability of the custom of washing women's feet based on this understanding. See *BCL Newsletter* 23 (1987): 53–54. The statement was authorized by the chairman of the BCL after a review of the matter by the committee.

[21]"Culture, Liturgy and," NDSW, 310.

[22]Most of the practices given here and elsewhere in this chapter were supplied to the author after coming to the attention of the staff of the Office for Divine Worship of the archdiocese of Chicago and the staff of Liturgy Training Publications. I am grateful for their assistance.

[23]A number of these practices have already been identified as abuses in Aidan Kavanagh, *Elements of Rite: A Handbook of Liturgical Style* (New York: Pueblo, 1982) and Dennis C. Smolarski, *How Not to Say Mass: A Guidebook for All Concerned About Authentic Worship* (New York/Mahwah, Paulist, 1986). The persistence of such abuses, despite strong criticism from liturgists, reinforces the need for the continuing liturgical formation of clergy and other liturgical ministers.

Preparation
for the Sacraments:
Faith, Rights, Law

Parish ministers and religious educators typically devote considerable time and energy to preparing parents for infant baptism, children for confirmation, first holy communion and first penance, and young adults for marriage. Anyone involved in this ministry knows that on the one hand, it can be very rewarding to see the expressions of faith and commitment of those about to receive a sacrament for the first time. On the other hand, many catechists and ministers experience feelings of frustration when dealing with Catholic people who want to receive a sacrament but are not registered in the parish, do not regularly attend Mass and want to avoid a catechetical program designed to prepare them to celebrate and receive the sacrament worthily.

The celebrations of baptism, confirmation, first holy communion, first penance and marriage are important occasions in the lives of the faithful. They are also important occasions in the life of the church community because the sacraments and other liturgical celebrations express the faith of the community and build it up. The church is the people of God, the body of Christ. The church's identity is revealed in a preeminent way at liturgy when it assembles in Christ's name to give praise and thanks to God. Those who celebrate the church's liturgies and request its sacraments should be people who have faith and are committed to their brothers and sisters in the community of the parish.

The liturgy, especially the sacraments, is central to the church's identity. Believing and committed Christians do not treat the sacraments lightly. They are sacred celebrations, intended for people of faith. In order to protect the integrity of the sacramental rites, canon law establishes certain requirements for participation in the liturgy and reception of the sacraments. The basic law is that only the baptized are admitted to the other sacraments (canon 842, §1). Those who are baptized are presumed to be believers; they are presumed to have faith. In virtue of their baptism they have a fundamental right in canon law to receive the sacraments. However, it is well known that there are many baptized persons whose faith is weak or altogether lacking. People baptized in infancy may not have been raised in the faith, may have abandoned the practice of the faith or may be lax in their practice of it. Yet even if faith is weak and the external practice of the faith is virtually nonexistent, the canonical right to the sacraments is not lost by the baptized. The right to the sacraments can be restricted only when permitted by law.

Faith, rights and law — all are involved in sacramental preparation and celebration. The first part of this essay is on the nature of faith: What is it? How does faith arise and develop? The second section considers two canons that speak of the relationship between faith and liturgy. The third section addresses the canonical right of the faithful to receive the sacraments. The fourth section treats select canonical norms on the preparation of parents and godparents for infant baptism, of children for the reception of confirmation, first eucharist and first penance, and of engaged couples for the sacrament of matrimony. The question of the necessary disposition to receive the sacraments, particularly the adequacy of one's faith, and the question of the right to the sacraments are considered in the course of the discussion of these canons on preparation for the sacraments.

Faith: Origins and Growth

There has not been a consensus in Christian tradition on how faith should be defined.[1] To some, faith is an intellectual assent; it is a property of the intellect, an affirmation of the dictates of reason and the truths and propositions revealed by God or declared as truths of the faith by the church. To others, faith is primarily affective, a child-like dependence upon and trust in the goodness of God. For others, faith is an act of the will, a free will choice to believe.

Faith is also spoken of as a gift, as primarily God's action. This notion of faith as a gift has been strongly rooted in Christian tradition since the epistle to the Ephesians: "For by grace you have been saved through faith, and this is not your own doing; it is the gift of God" (2:8). Faith cannot be understood as a gift in the ordinary sense of the word "gift," however. If faith is simply a gift, why does God give this gift only to some people but not to all people? Why are some members of the same family ardent believers, and others are complacent, agnostic or even hostile toward religion? If faith is solely a gratuitous gift from God, then God is capricious and arbitrary, dispensing the gift of faith to some and not to others. But this is not the loving and gracious God of revelation.

If the origins of faith cannot be explained as purely supernatural phenomena, then how does faith come about? What does it mean to say that someone has faith? It is more precise to say that faith is a response to grace. Grace is the gift from God which helps faith grow and deepen. Grace is God's gift. Faith is the response of human beings to this gift. Only in this sense is faith a gift from God, but a person "necessarily receives the gift of faith (or any gift from any source) according to his or her own nature and operations as a human being."[2] Human beings respond with their free will to the invitation to faith that God offers them through grace, in accord with their own nature.

For some time a distinction has been made between faith and belief.[3] Not everyone who expresses belief in God has authentic faith. Surveys show that 95 percent of people in the United States assert that they believe in God, though only 40 to 50 percent claim to attend services at their church every week. The actual figure is more likely about 28 percent.[4] There is a considerable difference between mere belief and a genuine faith that actually influences personal behavior.

Faith is not simply saying yes to the question, "Do you believe in God?" Faith is not a simple concept at all. If it were, it would be easy to define, easy to learn, and once learned, mastered for life. Faith is not a concept but a construct referring to a whole set of beliefs, values and behaviors. This construct is made even more complex by variables such as an individual's genetic makeup, personality, perception, intellect, knowledge, emotions and free will.[5] All of these factors come into play in determining who has faith and who does not.

Free will is an important aspect of personal faith. One's response to the divine invitation to faith is not entirely determined by genetic or environmental factors. If it were, there would be far fewer cases where in the same family some members have faith and others do not, where some are weekly communicants and others go to church only at Christmas and Easter. Faith development requires the individual's personal response. Each person must choose to observe the obligations that come with being a believer. God has given human beings free will; God also gives the grace for people to grow in faith if they respond willingly. However, to respond at all they must first learn about God; they must grow in knowledge of those beliefs, values and behaviors that together comprise the construct of faith.

This raises a related question. If faith is not purely a supernatural gift, then how is it acquired? In fact, it is learned. Except for innate responses like reflexes and other biological behaviors, human behavior is learned behavior. Anything that comes from culture, from one's social environment, is learned; faith is no exception. Learning begins in infancy and continues throughout life.

To say that faith is learned does not mean that it is learned primarily in the classroom. That is only one kind of learning. Learning takes place all the time in all kinds of settings. Young children are constantly learning new things about the world in which they have been born. Faith can be learned by experiencing activities that are part of the construct of faith, for example, by engaging in works of charity or justice, by prayer, by fasting, by participating in the liturgy.

Faith is like a young plant. It must be tended, watered and given nutrients. But even when a plant grows up, it still needs regular watering and fertilizing. Faith also needs continual nurturing throughout life. Faith always needs development and constant attention — through daily prayer, Bible study and spiritual reading, retreats and courses on religion, and most especially by regular worship with the faith community.[6] Faith grows by the practice of faith. The more one is exposed to catechesis, preaching and study, the more one consciously performs deeds of charity and justice in the name of faith; the more one prays daily and comes together with the community of faith for worship, the more will one's faith be deepened.

Faith is much more likely to develop when it is practiced regularly; but this does not always occur. People who attend Mass every Sunday might do so out of mere routine or social convention or due to neurotic, rather than authentic, guilt. Nor is it always true that the more one learns about one's faith, the stronger one's faith will be. A simple, uneducated person can have deep faith. In contrast, there are some professors of theology, priests and religious who devote nearly all of their professional lives to the subject or practice of religion but for whom it is merely an occupation; their faith has been lost somewhere on life's journey, and now they just go through the motions of external practice out of a sense of duty and without inner conviction. There are no simple rules for determining the quality and quantity of another person's faith. Personal faith is too complex to be easily measured or evaluated.

This first section can be summarized with five points:

(1) Faith is a complex construct, not a simple concept.
(2) Faith, like other forms of human behavior, is learned.

37

(3) Faith is not something that can be learned and mastered once and for all; it takes regular practice and new learning.

(4) Faith requires more than intellectual knowledge; it requires a free will response.

(5) It is not possible to know the quantity or quality of another person's faith; faith is an inner, spiritual reality, and mere external behavior is not a completely reliable indicator of a person's faith.

Faith and Liturgy: Canons 836 and 840

Canons 836 and 840 are at the beginning of Book IV of the *Code of Canon Law,* on the sanctifying office of the church. Canon 836 says, in part, that the liturgy "proceeds from faith and is based on [faith]." Because the liturgy is an expression of the community's faith, the canon exhorts ordained ministers "to strive diligently to arouse and enlighten that faith, especially through the ministry of the Word by which faith is born and nourished."[7] Ordained ministers are charged with helping people to develop their faith, and the principal way they are to do this is through the ministry of the word because, as the canon says, faith is born and nourished by the ministry of the word.

Faith is born by the ministry of the word and is nourished by the ministry of the word. Faith is supernatural in the sense that faith is born and grows as a response to God's grace. But God's grace works through people — it is incarnational, sacramental. God's grace is mediated by the church through the church's ministers and catechists, and by the domestic church through Christian parents who take seriously their obligation to bring up their children in the faith.

The ministry of the word is defined clearly in present canon law. Most of Book III of the code is devoted to it. The first section of Book III is called "The Ministry of the Divine Word," and it treats in particular the ministries of preaching and catechetics. Of the various forms of the ministry of the divine word, preaching and catechetical instruction are considered the most important. These are the primary ways that the ministry of the word is exercised and therefore the primary way that "faith is born and nourished."

Canon 761 in Book III speaks of some other forms of the ministry of the word: Catholic education in Catholic schools and universities, evangelization by missionaries and communication of the Christian message by means of books and other media. All of these are ways by which the beliefs, values and behaviors that make up the construct of faith are communicated to Christian people precisely to help them grow in faith. The implication of canon 836 is that the more the faithful are engaged in these faith-building activities, the more deeply they will be disposed to celebrate the church's liturgy worthily and fruitfully.

Canon 836 deals with the relationship of faith to liturgy. It refers to the expression of faith by the faith-filled community assembled for worship. Liturgical celebrations not only express faith, they strengthen faith. This is stated explicitly in reference to the sacraments in canon 840: Sacraments are "actions of Christ and of the church, they are signs and means by which faith is expressed and strengthened."[8] The Bishops' Committee on the Liturgy of the National Conference of Catholic Bishops (United States) states the matter forcefully: "Faith grows when it is well expressed in celebration. Good celebrations foster and nourish faith. Poor celebrations may weaken and destroy it."[9] Even people whose faith is nascent, weak or undeveloped can be inspired by a liturgical celebration to greater participation in the church's life and to an increase in their faith.

The postconciliar liturgical rites were designed to have one or more readings from the scriptures. Frequently, preaching is part of liturgical celebrations, particularly in the eucharist at which the homilist applies the scriptures to the everyday life of the listeners. At the liturgy of the word, faith is nurtured by the ministry of the word; it is nourished by the assembly itself as it expresses its common faith by gathering as God's holy people; faith is nourished through the ministry of the lectors who proclaim the word with faith, by cantors and choir who lift up the spirits of the assembly in song and by the homilist who explains the scriptural texts and relates them to the paschal mysteries.

The Right to the Sacraments

There is a close relationship between faith and liturgy. The liturgy presupposes faith, but it also builds up faith. Sometimes, however, people who seemingly lack sufficient faith and commitment to the church approach the sacraments. These "marginal Catholics," as they have been called, are persons who, though they are fully initiated members of the church, are seriously deficient in the external practice of their faith.[10] Those involved in pastoral ministry have to consider the serious questions raised by the presence of marginal Catholics. Should such persons be denied sacramental celebrations, such as a wedding or the baptism of their child? When may, or when should, the church's ministers deny sacraments to persons if they are perceived to lack sufficient faith? How do ministers make such judgments? What legal basis do they have for their decisions?

As will be demonstrated, only in rare cases does canon law enable a minister to refuse or to delay reception of a sacrament to a baptized Catholic. There is a theological reason for this caution in the law. As seen in canon 840 above, "faith is expressed and strengthened" by the sacraments. When the faithful request a sacrament, even if they do not regularly practice their faith, it can usually be presumed that they have some degree of faith or else they would not be seeking the sacrament. Through the preparation for and celebration of a special sacramental moment in their lives, God's grace can touch the hearts of such people and move them to respond to this grace by practicing their religion with greater fidelity.

The right to the sacraments is expressed in canon 213: "The Christian faithful have the right to receive assistance from the sacred pastors out of the spiritual goods of the church, especially the word of God and the sacraments." This is a fundamental right of the faithful that appears with other basic rights and duties enumerated at the beginning of Book II of the code. The fact that there is a canonical right to the word of God and the sacraments implies an obligation on the part of pastors to provide it. Rights and duties go hand in hand in canon law. If someone has a right to something, generally there is a complementary obligation on an office-holder to ensure the fulfillment of this right. If the right to word and sacrament is to be realized, the ministers of word and sacrament have a duty to exercise their ministry as the law requires.

Canon 843, §1 flows directly from the right of the faithful to word and sacrament. It states: "The sacred ministers cannot refuse the sacraments to those who ask for them at appropriate times, are properly disposed and are not prohibited by law from receiving them." The law speaks of denial of a sacrament, but this is not an absolute denial of a right. It must be understood as a temporary denial, or delay, until the person in question fulfills the requirements of the law. It may happen that the person never fulfills these requirements, but the fundamental right to the sacrament by the baptized cannot be lost completely. Even persons who commit a grave crime and are publicly excommunicated must be readmitted to the sacraments if they repent and the penalty is remitted (canon 1358).

According to canon 843, §1, there are three general reasons why a sacrament may be denied or, better put, delayed. The first reason is someone requesting a sacrament at a time that is not opportune or appropriate. The appropriate time could refer to the liturgical season, the time of day or the actual moment of reception.[11] For example, several people ask to go to confession just as Mass is about to begin, and the priest judges that to delay Mass would be harmful to the common good. The priest could invite these people to return to him after Mass, reminding them that they can receive holy communion at that Mass, even if they are in serious sin, if they have a grave reason for doing so and make an act of perfect contrition with the intention of confessing their serious sins as soon as possible (canon 916).

The second reason given in canon 843, §1 for delaying a sacrament occurs when a person lacks the proper disposition. For example, a confessor determines that a penitent is not sorry for a sin confessed because he or she does not believe the act to be sinful. The confessor should delay absolution until the penitent shows some sign of contrition.

The third reason for denying or delaying a sacrament occurs when the law prohibits reception. There are many laws regulating access to the sacraments. An example is canon 918, which says that a person who wishes to receive holy communion outside of Mass must have a just cause for requesting it, for example, illness or old age. Without such a just cause, the minister should refuse the sacrament in order to protect the value that holy communion is optimally received during the eucharistic celebration.

This second requirement — the need for a proper disposition — is the most germane to the issues at hand. The requirement of a proper disposition to receive the sacraments includes the need for a sufficient faith to be open to the grace of the sacraments. But one's disposition for receiving a sacrament is an interior, spiritual reality. Usually the minister has no idea at all of the interior disposition of a person. Hundreds of people receive holy communion in a typical parish each Sunday. The ministers of communion can hardly be expected to know the disposition of each one of them. On the other hand, in the sacrament of penance or in the course of marriage preparation, the minister can more readily make a determination about whether someone has the proper disposition for the sacrament. Any doubts about the proper disposition should be resolved in favor of the person's request to receive a sacrament.[12]

Canon law requires a strict interpretation of the law whenever some legal right is at stake (canon 18). In reference to the denial of a sacrament, this means that ministers are not free to impose their own standards for sacramental reception. A sacrament may only be denied for a reason stated in the law.

Preparation for the Sacraments

Faith is born and is nourished by the ministry of the word and by participation in faith activities, especially the church's liturgy. The baptized have a fundamental right to the word of God and the sacraments, and ordained ministers have the obligation to administer the sacraments, provided people ask for the sacraments at an opportune time, are properly disposed and are not prohibited by law from receiving them. This section will consider select canons from the code on preparation for the sacraments, especially canons that are related to the need for sufficient faith and the proper disposition for the sacrament. In particular, two questions are addressed: Can Catholics be denied a particular sacrament by a minister who judges that they have insufficient faith? And, can Catholics who are otherwise eligible to receive a sacrament be denied a sacrament because they cannot or do not want to participate in a sacramental preparation program?

The faithful have a right to receive the sacraments, and they also have a right to receive preparation for the sacraments. This right is implied in the second paragraph of canon 843, which states: "Pastors of souls and the rest of the Christian faithful, according to their ecclesial function, have the duty to see that those who seek the sacraments are prepared to receive them by the necessary evangelization and catechetical formation, taking into account the norms published by competent authority." Because the law imposes a duty on pastors of souls and other members of the faithful to provide sacramental preparation, there is an implied right of the faithful to have access to this preparation. The burden of the law does not fall on the faithful. The law does not say that they must have such preparation before they can receive a sacrament. The law imposes the duty on the church's ministers to provide this preparation.

As noted above in reference to canon 836, the ministry of the word is an essential means of nurturing faith and preparing the faithful for a fruitful celebration of the liturgy. Canon 843, §2 addresses precisely this point, and it imposes the duty upon the church's pastors and other members of the faithful — including teachers of religion and others who have pastoral offices — to ensure that the faithful have adequate preparation for the sacraments by means of evangelization and catechetical instruction.

The faithful have the right to this formation, but it does not necessarily follow that they may be denied the reception of a sacrament because they fail to exercise their right to have adequate preparation. To determine whether a sacrament can be denied on the basis of lack of preparation, the minister must look at the legal requirements governing preparation for the reception of the various sacraments. The remainder of this chapter will examine select norms on preparation for the sacraments of baptism, confirmation, eucharist and marriage.

Infant Baptism

Canon 851, 2° speaks in general terms of the preparation of
parents and godparents:

> It is necessary that the celebration of baptism be properly prepared. Thus
> the parents of an infant who is to be baptized and likewise those who are to
> undertake the office of sponsor are to be properly instructed in the mean-
> ing of this sacrament and the obligations which are attached to it; personally
> or through others the pastor is to see to it that the parents are properly
> formed by pastoral directions and by common prayer, gathering several
> families together and where possible visiting them.[13]

The pastor is charged with the duty of seeing that suitable catechetical and spiritual preparation is provided. The parents and
godparents should take part in the preparation program that
the parish provides as a general rule; but the law does not lay
down an absolute command. It does not use a strongly preceptive
verb like "must" or "is required." It uses exhortative language.
The parents and godparents of a child who is to be baptized "are
to receive" suitable instruction. This kind of language is common in canon law whenever the law speaks of the best way that
something ought to be done. To express these kinds of values
the law uses "should" statements, not "must" statements. While
still obligatory, this milder kind of legal language more easily
admits exception than would a law that uses a strong command.

There are reasons that would excuse from observing this
law. These include godparents who live far from the parish and
would otherwise be inconvenienced by being compelled to
participate; parents who work at the time the preparation program
is held; parents who not long ago went through the preparation
program for a previous child. As for non-Catholic parents or
non-Catholic witnesses to the baptism, they should be invited to
participate in the program, but they would be under no obligation,
because canon law binds only Catholics (canon 11).

As a rule, parents ought to have more serious reasons than
godparents for not taking part in the preparation program.
Parents have the primary responsibility for raising the child in
the faith; godparents usually do not exercise this role directly.
Although not the ideal, it would suffice if at least one parent

underwent the preparation program; but for good reason, even this could be excused. If neither parent can attend, the pastor or other minister in charge of the baptismal program can judge whether the reason given by the parents is sufficient to excuse from the standard preparation program of the parish. If the parents are unable to attend a catechetical session at a certain time, it is still the pastor's duty to see that they are given suitable instruction on the meaning of this sacrament and on their obligations. He may have to provide a special session to accommodate their needs. In addition, the homily at the baptismal liturgy can be an opportunity for instruction about the meaning of the sacrament and about the duties of Christian parents and godparents (RBC, 17, 45).

What if neither parent has a convincing reason for not coming to the baptismal preparation program and the parents refuse all efforts by the pastor to accommodate them? Should the infant's baptism be denied? Canon 868, §1 gives the rule for delay of baptism: "For the licit baptism of an infant it is necessary that (1) the parents or at least one of them or the person who lawfully takes their place gives consent; (2) there be a founded hope that the infant will be brought up in the Catholic religion; if such a hope is altogether lacking, the baptism is to be put off according to the prescriptions of particular law and the parents are to be informed of the reason."[14] The law requires that there be a "founded hope" that the child will be brought up in the Catholic faith. This means that there is some basis, some reason, for the hope. If parents altogether refuse to become involved in the parish's preparation program, it may be an indication of a deeper faith problem that could warrant delay of baptism. Some major signs of such a problem are: when parents have a purely extraneous reason for wanting the child baptized, for example, to please their own parents and keep peace in the family; when parents have a hostile attitude toward the Catholic faith or to religion in general; when parents admit they have no intention of ever practicing the faith; when they refuse or are reluctant to acknowledge that they have the obligation to raise the child in the faith.

These attitudes may indicate that baptism may need to be deferred until at least one of the parents exhibits a change of heart. Such persons greatly need catechesis on their obligations as Christian parents. If parents who themselves lack the faith completely refuse, without valid reasons, to participate in any kind of catechesis and remain adamant and hostile, the minister should politely and sensitively explain why baptism will have to be deferred. The church does not consider baptism a magical act or merely a nice ceremony it provides for newborn babies. It is the celebration of faith and of entrance into the faith community; it is a faith that will need to be nurtured in childhood primarily under the parents' direction. There must be some minimal indication, some "founded hope," that the child will be raised in the faith.

If the parents cannot offer this minimal hope, it is possible that someone else could undertake the responsibility of seeing to the child's Christian upbringing — a godparent or grandparent, for example. But in this case there must be an assurance that the parents will not block the effort.

Cases where infant baptism should be delayed are rare. Most parents, even if they are not regularly practicing their faith, have some minimal faith themselves and desire baptism for their child. They should not be required to register in the parish or begin going to Sunday Mass as conditions for the baptism of their child. They should be invited, exhorted and encouraged to do so, but the minister can only delay the sacrament for the reason given in the law. Parish registration and weekly Mass attendance are not legal requirements for the reception of sacraments. It is only when, in the words of canon 868, a founded hope is "altogether lacking" that the baptism is to be deferred. In such a case, the minister must explain to the parents why baptism is being deferred and tell them under what conditions baptism can later be granted. If there are any local policies on this matter, they too must be observed.[15]

Confirmation

Confirmation is the second sacrament of initiation, normatively celebrated after baptism and before first eucharist,[16] although in most places in North America this proper sequence is not observed by the Latin church. The universal law of the Latin church says that confirmation should be conferred "at about the age of discretion," that is, at about seven years of age (canon 891). Ideally, as the Rite of Confirmation exhorts, the celebration of confirmation should take place during the eucharistic celebration at which the newly confirmed complete their Christian initiation by being admitted to holy communion for the first time (RC, 13). If the bishop personally cannot administer confirmation to all the children in the diocese on the occasion of first holy communion, he may give the faculty to confirm to specified presbyters so that they may do it (canon 884, §1).[17]

Because canon law considers young children to be fit subjects for confirmation, it understandably imposes minimal requirements for reception of the sacrament. According to canon 889, §2: "Outside of the danger of death, to be licitly confirmed it is required, if the person has the use of reason, that one be suitably instructed, properly disposed and able to renew one's baptismal promises." If the person lacks the use of reason or there is danger of death, there are no requirements at all for confirmation other than that the person be baptized. Thus, an infant in danger of death can and should be confirmed. Or persons who are seven or older but lack the use of reason due to a developmental disability (such as mental retardation) can and should be confirmed. No preparation, catechesis or renewal of baptismal promises is needed.[18]

The proper disposition to receive confirmation includes being in the state of grace (RC, 12). Baptized persons with the use of reason who have committed mortal sin should make a sacramental confession before confirmation. The minister can presume sufficient disposition in young children and adults who have been given suitable instruction, including an admonition that they be in the state of grace.

The liturgical law leaves it to the conference of bishops to determine more precisely the meaning of "suitable instruction"

in the case of children.[19] However, the principal responsibility
for a child's preparation is assigned to the parents:

> The initiation of children into the sacramental life is ordinarily the
> responsibility and concern of Christian parents. They are to form and
> gradually increase a spirit of faith in the children and, at times with
> the help of catechism classes, prepare them for the fruitful reception of the
> sacraments of confirmation and eucharist. The role of the parents is also
> expressed by their active participation in the celebration of the sacraments.[20]

This is in keeping with common norms from the code governing
catechesis: Parents have the primary responsibility for cate-
chizing their children (canons 774, §2; 226, §2; 793); pastors
of souls, especially pastors of parishes, have the secondary
responsibility (canons 773, 776). Catechesis for confirmation
should aim to be a positive experience to build up the faith
of the *confirmandi* and should not be perceived in a negative
way as merely a legal requirement that children must endure
if they want to receive the sacrament.

Although some suitable instruction before confirmation is ordinarily required, there is no basis in the universal law for denying
confirmation to a child who does not participate completely
in the precise program that the parish or school has established.
The law does not require a lengthy program of instruction,
service projects, retreats or other quite specific means of catechesis and formation. It only requires instruction suitable to the
level of a young child.

There are times when a child is not able to participate fully
or even partially in the regular confirmation preparation program.
In such a case, alternative catechesis should be provided, or
at least the parents should be reminded of their responsibility in
this regard. Minimally, the catechesis should aim to help the
children understand that confirmation is a sacrament of initiation
and that its true meaning is to be found in relation to Christian
initiation and the other sacraments of initiation. Catechesis also
ought to be given on the mysteries affirmed in the baptismal
promises, since the renewal of baptismal promises is a part of
the rite itself (RC, 23).

This is not meant to recommend a minimalist approach to catechesis or to denigrate the extended and highly structured confirmation programs that are found in Catholic parishes and schools

in North America. Surely, such preparation is useful and helpful, and ought to be an aid in the growth of the child's faith. But failure to participate in or complete the program cannot be used as the sole reason for refusing the sacrament.[21]

First Penance and First Communion

The requirements for the reception of first communion are not excessive, but they are more demanding than the minimal requirements set for confirmation.

> Canon 913, §1. For the administration of the Most Holy Eucharist to children, it is required that they have sufficient knowledge and careful preparation so as to understand the mystery of Christ according to their capacity, and can receive the Body of the Lord with faith and devotion.
>
> § 2. The Most Holy Eucharist may be given to children who are in danger of death, however, if they are able to distinguish the Body of Christ from ordinary food and to receive communion reverently.
>
> Canon 914. It is the responsibility, in the first place, of parents and those who take the place of parents as well as of the pastor to see that children who have reached the use of reason are correctly prepared and are nourished by the divine food as early as possible, preceded by sacramental confession; it is also for the pastor to be vigilant lest any children come to the Holy Banquet who have not reached the use of reason or whom he judges are not sufficiently disposed.

The appropriate time for the celebration of first communion is the age of reason, which in the law is presumed to be about the age of seven (canon 97, §2). Canon 914, which is directed to parents and pastors, obliges them to see that children who have reached the use of reason receive holy communion as soon as possible.

Canon 913 describes in general terms the "sufficient knowledge" and "accurate preparation" necessary for first communion. The children must be able to have some understanding, "according to their capacity," of the mystery they are celebrating, and they must be able to receive holy communion with faith and devotion. Minimally, they must be able to distinguish the body of Christ from ordinary food and receive communion reverently.

These requirements pose few pastoral problems. Rarely is a child denied first communion for lack of sufficient knowledge, faith or devotion. Unfortunately, what does occur in some places is the improper application of these requirements — which are intended for children who enjoy normal development — to persons with developmental disabilities. There are solid theological, psychological and canonical reasons in support of admitting persons with developmental disabilities such as mental retardation to the eucharistic banquet.[22] To deny such baptized persons the sacraments of confirmation, eucharist and penance is to deny their full personhood as children of God and members of the body of Christ. Some parishes and dioceses offer special religious education classes for these children. This is a good way to respond to the requirement of canon 777, 4°, which says that the pastor is to see that catechetical formation is given to those handicapped in body or mind insofar as their condition permits.

It is important to recognize that the parents are not required by canon law to participate in sacramental preparation programs along with their children. While this is doubtless an excellent formative experience for both parents and children, a child cannot be denied holy communion (or the sacraments of confirmation or penance) because his or her parents do not participate in the catechetical program. That is a violation of the child's right to the sacraments.

An issue related to the proper disposition for first communion is the requirement of canon 914 that children make a sacramental confession before first holy communion.[23] While this requirement urges in the normal case, there may be situations when a child, with the support of his or her parents, is not ready or willing to approach the sacrament of penance at the age of seven. If these children have the proper disposition and are in the state of grace, they can and should be admitted to first communion even if they have not made their first confession. Canon 914 establishes an obligation for parents and pastors; it is they who are addressed in the canon, not young children. Pastors and parents are obliged to offer children suitable preparation for the sacrament of penance before their first communion so that the children have a realistic opportunity to avail themselves of the sacrament of penance. However, a child should not be denied the eucharist if he or she chooses not to make use of the right to the sacrament of penance.[24] The church's long-standing tradition is that only those in serious sin are excluded from the eucharist (canons 915, 916, 960, 988).

Some preparation for the sacraments of first penance and first eucharist is necessary if a child, in the normal situation, is to be admitted to these sacraments. However, it does not have to be the specific catechetical preparation offered by the parish for all children. Exceptions to this program should be permitted when there are good reasons. Some families are not registered in any parish because they have no domicile or quasi-domicile. For legal purposes, their parish is whatever parish they are staying in at the time (canon 107, §2). A baptized Catholic child of such parents can and should be admitted to the sacraments of confirmation, eucharist and penance in the parish where they are staying, even if they are unable to go through the complete catechetical process offered to other children. There would need to be some minimal instruction so that they are able to under-stand the meaning of these sacraments according to their capacity and to celebrate and receive them properly. However, the specific catechetical program of the parish for those sacraments need not be observed in all instances.

It is helpful for ministers and catechists to realize that parents have the right and obligation to be the primary educators of children in the faith (canon 226, §2). If parents give good reasons why their child cannot participate fully in the parish sacramental preparation program, the pastor should instruct the parents of their own duty to see that adequate preparation is provided either by them or by someone else who is willing to undertake this responsibility. This relieves the pastor or catechetical director of the sole burden of judging who is and who is not worthy of receiving the sacraments.

Marriage

Marriage between two baptized persons is a sacrament (canon 1055). Because it is a sacrament, some minimal level of faith must exist if the grace of the sacrament is to have an effect.[25] The code does not explicitly treat the relationship between faith and preparation for marriage, but there is a norm addressing this issue in the Rite of Celebrating Marriage. The 1990 revised rite states: "Pastors, led by the love of Christ, should draw out the faith of those to be married and especially should strengthen and nourish their faith, for the sacrament of matrimony presupposes and demands faith" (16).

This law is directed to the church's ministers, not to the couple. It does not say that the couple has to demonstrate the adequacy of their faith to the satisfaction of the priest. It presumes the couple has faith to some degree and therefore obliges pastors to draw it out from them, to strengthen it and nourish it. Their faith, however minimal, should be strengthened and nourished during the course of the marriage preparation.

People between the ages of 18 and 34, the time when most people marry, are the least likely of any age group to attend church services regularly.[26] Many cease participating in their religion at this age only to return later, when their own children go to school. The lack of practice at that age should not be equated with a lack of faith. Young adults generally have religious feelings and beliefs, but at this point in their lives, they often lack a sense of personal commitment to organized religion.

Should a sacramental marriage ever be denied on the basis of lack of faith? If the parties admit they have no faith at all, it would be better to dissuade the couple from marrying in the church. However, such a frank confession of lack of faith is very unlikely to occur. More commonly, one or both parties simply do not practice their faith. The mere lack of the external observance of religion, however, is not a reason for denying a couple the sacrament of marriage.

Even if faith is completely absent in both parties, they could still celebrate the sacrament of marriage validly.[27] The presence or absence of faith does not in itself make a sacramental marriage valid or invalid, but if there is no faith at all, the validity of the sacrament is "compromised."[28] The husband and wife are the ministers of the sacrament. As ministers, they must have the proper intention to celebrate the sacrament validly. They must intend to do what the church does. Minimally, they must not place an obstacle to the grace of the sacrament; they must not have a positive intention against the sacramentality of marriage. Even Protestants, who do not believe that marriage is a sacrament, receive the sacrament validly because ordinarily they do not have a positive intention against sacramentality when they give their consent. Their belief that marriage is not a sacrament is presumed to affect only their intellect but not their will (canon 1099). Their consent is defective only if they positively intend not to have a sacramental union.

Catholics, even those who do not practice the faith, have a right to marry in the church. This right to a Catholic marriage can be restricted only for reasons specified in the law. The fact that one or both parties do not practice their faith is not a legal reason for refusing them the sacrament. On the contrary, the preparation for and celebration of Christian marriage, when done well, can be an important way to keep young people in the church and inspire in them the desire to practice their faith with regularity.

Marriage Preparation

Since faith is learned from faith-building experiences, a good marriage preparation program is an excellent way to build up the faith of young couples. As part of their preparation for marriage, canon law strongly recommends that they approach the sacraments of penance and holy eucharist so that they are in the state of grace when they marry (canon 1065, §2).

Canon 1063 is the principal canon devoted to the topic of marriage preparation. It is addressed to pastoral ministers and obliges them to see that formation in Christian marriage is provided in four ways: (1) through preaching, catechetical instruction and the means of social communication in order to teach about the meaning of Christian marriage and the role of Christian spouses and parents; (2) through the more immediate personal preparation of the engaged couple; (3) through the fruitful celebration of the marriage liturgy; and (4) through continuing assistance given to married couples.

Canon 1063 deals with three levels of formation for marriage. The first level is the remote preparation given to minors, youths and adults. The third level is the ongoing assistance given to married couples. The second level, treated in paragraphs 2 and 3 of the canon, applies to engaged couples. Paragraph 2 speaks of "personal preparation for entering marriage so that through such preparation the parties may be predisposed toward the holiness and duties of their new state." Paragraph 3 calls for "a fruitful liturgical celebration of marriage clarifying that the spouses signify and share in that mystery of unity and of fruitful love that exists between Christ and the church." A good marriage preparation program and an effective liturgical celebration of marriage can increase the faith of the couple. A positive experience at this stage can lead parties who have been lax to a more regular practice of their faith.

A couple not practicing the faith regularly but willing to observe the marriage preparation program of the parish should not be prevented from marrying in the church. But what if they are not willing to go through a marriage preparation program? Is preparation for the sacrament of marriage a *sine qua non?* Or is it only a pastoral option?

In introducing the kinds of formation for marriage, canon 1063 states that pastors of souls are obliged to ensure that this formation is provided. The obligation is not addressed to the parties who wish to marry. The code leaves it to local churches — to conferences of bishops and to dioceses — to develop more specific policies regulating marriage preparation (canons 1067, 1064, 1077). In most dioceses in the United States a marriage preparation program is required.[29] If a couple refuses any kind of marriage preparation, their marriage can be delayed, provided such a delay is permitted by the local ordinary either for that case or as a general policy. Canon 1077, §1 is the legal basis for those marriage preparation programs that permit the delay of marriage in cases where couples lack the necessary disposition or readiness.

If marriage preparation programs are mandatory, it is all the more important that they be done well so that reluctant participants have a positive experience. However, even mandatory programs should admit of exceptions for people who cannot attend the sessions. There are situations in which one or both parties to the marriage have a good excuse for not taking the standard marriage preparation program. For example, one or both of them must work at the time the program is given. One of them may be in the military and is stationed elsewhere or is a student attending a university out of town. It might be a second marriage for both of them, and thus certain segments of the marriage preparation program would not apply in their situation. Local policies must be flexible enough to accommodate the genuine needs of such persons. Pastors may have to adapt or shorten the marriage preparation program to fit their needs.[30]

Conclusion

Faith results from learning, but it also requires a free will response to the grace that God offers through the church, especially through the liturgy. Faith grows by the practice of faith; it is nourished by the ministry of the word, by the liturgy and by other faith activities. But learning about faith and the experience of faith activities do not guarantee that faith will grow or will always be sustained by everyone. A person can observe the external requirements of religion while withholding the free will assent to God's grace that is essential for a genuine faith. Likewise, people can have minimal faith at one stage in their life but be inspired later in life to deepen their faith and come to a regular practice of it. It is precisely at special sacramental moments like a marriage or the baptism of a child that this phenomenon frequently occurs.

Some priests, deacons and lay ministers are overly zealous in their efforts to protect the integrity of the sacraments from "marginal" Catholics. They want to make sure that no one comes to the sacraments who has insufficient faith. Their judgments about lack of faith in other people are usually made on the basis of external criteria, notably lack of participation in the Sunday eucharist. Ironically, by denying a couple a Catholic wedding, a baptism for their child or some other sacrament or rite, overly zealous ministers may be missing an opportunity to enable the grace of the sacraments to increase the participants' faith. They can unwittingly be responsible for alienating persons of weak faith and destroying the chance for their faith to grow.

Sacraments not only presuppose personal faith, they also build up faith. The baptized have a fundamental right to receive the word of God and the sacraments, and the church's ministers may not refuse them a sacrament except for a reason given in the law. When a sacramental celebration is denied to those weak in faith or to those who do not regularly practice the faith, they may be deprived of divine grace, which could be the very means to help them grow in faith and in their practice of it.

NOTES

[1]See Monika K. Hellwig, "A History of the Concept of Faith," in *Handbook of Faith,* ed. James M. Lee (Birmingham, AL: Religious Education Press, 1990): 3–23.

[2]James M. Lee, "Facilitating Faith Through Religious Instruction," *Handbook of Faith,* 271.

[3]See, for example, Gordon Allport, *The Individual and His Religion: A Psychological Interpretation* (New York: Macmillan, 1950; paperback edition, 1960): 140–41. Allport recognized that "faith is probably more complex psychologically than is simple belief."

[4]These figures are based on individuals' own self-reporting; Catholics, at 43 percent, attend church weekly at about the same rate as non-Catholics. See the results of the Gallup poll reported in *National Catholic Reporter* (October 8, 1993): 26. In fact, the actual weekly Mass attendance figure for Catholics is more likely about 28 percent. The higher figure results from respondents who want to create a more favorable impression of themselves. See Mark Chaves and James C. Cavendish, "More Evidence on U.S. Catholic Church Attendance," *Journal for the Scientific Study of Religion* 33 (1994): 376–81. This latter study used data indicating a 50 percent weekly attendance figure based on Catholics' self-reporting.

[5]See James W. Fowler, *Faith Development and Pastoral Care,* Theology and Pastoral Care Series (Philadelphia: Fortress Press, 1987): 102.

[6]Canon law implicitly recognizes this concern. See canons 246, 276, 663, 664, 719, 1247. See also James W. Fowler, *Becoming Adult, Becoming Christian: Adult Development and Christian Faith* (San Francisco: Harper & Row, 1984).

[7]See also SC, 9–11, 33, 59.

[8]See also SC, 26, 59.

[9]*Music in Catholic Worship,* 6 (Washington: USCC, 1972). This document also appears with a commentary by Edward Foley in *The Liturgy Documents: A Parish Resource,* 3rd edition (Chicago: Liturgy Training Publications, 1991): 269–94.

[10]Joseph M. Champlin, *The Marginal Catholic: Challenge, Don't Crush* (Notre Dame, IN: University of Notre Dame Press, 1989). This book is an excellent treatment of this complex pastoral question. See also Bishop John McCarthy, "On Refusing Sacraments to 'Nominal' Catholics," *Origins* 22 (1992–1993): 392–94.

[11]Francis G. Morrisey, "Denial of a Sacrament Without Due Process," *Roman Replies and CLSA Advisory Opinions 1991* (Washington: CLSA, 1991): 88.

[12]Frederick R. McManus observes: "[T]he proper disposition or faith and devotion can be judged adequately only by the person who seeks the sacrament. Although a judgment can and sometimes must be made by the minister, the canon establishes a presumption in favor of the Christian person." See "Introduction to Book IV," in *The Code of Canon Law: A Text and Commentary,* ed. James A. Coriden, Thomas J. Green, and Donald E. Heintschel (New York, Mahwah, NJ: Paulist, 1985): 609.

[13]See also Rite of Baptism for Children (RBC), 5.1. The CLSA translation renders *patrinus* as "sponsor," but the approved translation in the rites is "godparent."

[14]See also CDF, Instruction on the Baptism of Children, October 20, 1980, AAS 72 (1980): 1137–1156.

[15]See B. Daly, "Canonical Requirements of Parents in Cases of Infant Baptism According to the 1983 Code," *Studia Canonica* 20 (1986): 409–38, especially 429–34. Daly quotes policies of various dioceses on what constitutes a "founded hope" and the circumstances that would call for a delay of infant baptism.

[16]The liturgical books and the code consistently treat the three sacraments of initiation in this order. Eucharist is seen as the culmination or completion of initiation.

[17]The lawfulness and pastoral utility of this interpretation of canon 884 is argued persuasively by R.J. Barrett in "Confirmation: A Discipline Revisited," *The Jurist* 52 (1992): 697–714.

[18]See my essay, "Canonical Rights to the Sacraments," in *Developmental Disabilities and Sacramental Access: New Paradigms for Sacramental Encounters,* ed. Edward Foley (Collegeville: Liturgical Press, 1994): 94–115.

[19]For adults, it recommends that elements of the RCIA be adapted for *confirmandi.* See RC, 12.

[20]RC, 3. See Francis G. Morrisey, "The Rights of Parents in the Education of their Children," *Studia Canonica* 23 (1989): 429–44; M.R. Quinlan, "Parental Rights and Admission of Children to the Sacraments of Initiation," *Studia Canonica* 25 (1991): 385–401. While parents have the primary responsibility for the catechesis of their children, the law also sees this as the duty of the church's ministers: "Pastors *(pastores)* have the special responsibility to see that all the baptized reach the completion of Christian initiation and therefore that they are carefully prepared for confirmation" (RC, 3). See also canon 890, which singles out parish priests *(parochi)* as among the pastors of souls who especially have the duty of seeing that the faithful are properly instructed to receive confirmation and to approach it at the appropriate time.

[21]I have heard of cases in which children were not approved for confirmation by their religion teacher because they failed to perform satisfactorily one or more aspects of the course. There should be some other way to get children to do their homework besides denying them a sacrament by which they "are enriched by the gift of the Holy Spirit and are bound more perfectly to the church" (canon 879).

[22]See Walter Kern, *Pastoral Ministry with Disabled Persons* (New York: Alba House, 1985); D. Wilson, "The Church, the Eucharist, and the Mentally Handicapped," *Clergy Review* 60 (1975): 69–84; *idem, L'Église, l'Eucharistie et les handicapés mentaux* (Lille: Fédération Universitaire et Polytechnique de Lille, Faculté de Théologie, 1974): 49–56; Urban Holmes, *Young Children and the Eucharist* (New York: Seabury, 1982); and note 17 above.

[23]See James H. Provost, "The Reception of First Penance," *The Jurist* 47 (1987): 294–340; John M. Huels, *Disputed Questions in the Liturgy Today* (Chicago: Liturgy Training Publications, 1988): 67–74; William H. Woestman, *Sacraments: Initiation, Penance, Anointing of the Sick* (Ottawa: Faculty of Canon Law, Saint Paul University, 1992): 129–31.

[24]This interpretation of canon 914 has been adopted as policy by the bishops of the ecclesiastical province of Chicago. Norm 34F states: "In those cases in which a child, because of exceptional reasons and under the guidance of his or her parents, chooses not to receive the sacrament of penance, he or she should not be deprived

of the right to make first holy communion. It is important that the child be encouraged to celebrate the sacrament of penance later so that he or she will not be deprived of it altogether." See *The Sacrament of Penance; Guidelines for the Dioceses of Illinois,* p. 6. The guidelines, dated November 27, 1988, were published by the Archdiocese of Chicago.

[25]See R.C. Finn, "Faith and the Sacrament of Marriage: General Conclusions from an Historical Study," *Marriage Studies III: Reflections in Canon Law and Theology,* ed. Thomas P. Doyle (Washington: CLSA, 1985): 95–111.

[26]The 1993 NCR/Gallup poll found that 24 percent of persons in this age group reported that they attended Mass once a week or more; it was 45 percent in the 35–54 age group, and 63 percent among those 55 and older. See *National Catholic Reporter* (October 8, 1993): 26.

[27]See Louis de Naurois, "Le mariage des baptisés qui n'ont pas la foi: aspects canoniques et soubassements théologiques du problème," *Foi et sacrement de mariage: recherche et perplexités* (Lyon: Chalet, 1974): 68–89. On page 83 de Naurois discusses this question. In the absence of faith, he says, the sacrament is valid but it does not produce its effect of grace. This grace comes to the person if the faith itself comes or returns. A sacrament "is" or "is not." Its validity cannot depend on an interior reality so difficult to define and to appreciate concretely as the interior disposition that is faith.

[28]The International Theological Commission concluded: "Where there is no trace of faith (in the sense of "belief" — being disposed to believe), and no desire for grace or salvation is found, then a real doubt arises as to whether there is the above-mentioned general and truly sacramental intention and whether the contracted marriage is validly contracted or not. As was noted, the personal faith of the contracting parties does not constitute the sacramentality of matrimony, but the absence of personal faith compromises the validity of the sacrament." See "Propositions on the Doctrine of Christian Marriage," *Origins* 8 (1978–1979): 237. For more on this question see Richard G. Cunningham, "Marriage and the Nescient Catholic: Questions of Faith and Sacrament," *Marriage Studies II* (Washington: CLSA, 1982): 20–37.

[29]A somewhat dated study found that over 90 percent of dioceses in the United States have marriage preparation policies, and over 60 percent of these are mandatory. See *Preparing for Marriage: A Study of Marriage Preparation in American Catholic Dioceses* (St. Meinrad, IN: Abbey Press, 1983): 15.

[30]For further treatment of marriage preparation and the issue of the couple's faith, see John Paul II, apostolic exhortation *Familiaris consortio,* 68, November 22, 1981, AAS 73 (1981): 81–191; English translation in *Origins* 11 (1981); Bishops' Committee for Pastoral Research and Practices, *Faithful to Each Other Forever: A Catholic Handbook of Pastoral Help for Marriage Preparation* (Washington: USCC, 1989) 60-63; Champlin, *The Marginal Catholic,* chapters 9-10; D. K. O'Rourke, "Unfair Assessments: Obstacles for Engaged Couples," *Church* (Fall 1985): 24–26; D. Neumann, "Realistic Expectations: Marriage Preparation in the Church Today," *Federation of Diocesan Liturgical Commissions Newsletter* 20 (March–April 1993): 11–15.

The Sunday Mass Obligation

Sociological research, based on the count of the actual number of people in church, reveals that only about 28 percent of Roman Catholics in the United States attend Mass on a given Sunday, although about 50 percent claim they do.[1] But it does not take a sociologist to demonstrate a fact that is well known to anyone with memories that go back to the 1960s and earlier: Today there are far fewer people going to Mass every Sunday than in the recent past. Scholars have offered a number of reasons for this decline. For example, Andrew Greeley is convinced on the basis of his research that Pope Paul VI's reaffirmation of papal opposition to artificial birth control in 1968 led to a precipitous and lasting decline in the Sunday observance.[2] Whatever the reasons, this decline has not been due to a change in canon law. The law is still substantially the same as it was before Vatican II, even though it is rarely preached and taught as forcefully as it once was.

The *Code of Canon Law* obliges all Catholics who are at least seven years of age and have the use of reason to participate in the celebration of the eucharist every Sunday and holy day of obligation, and to refrain from unnecessary, arduous work on these days. This essay looks at one part of this precept, that requiring attendance at Sunday Mass. We shall first outline the history of the Sunday Mass obligation: a matter regulated in some places by local legislation, then gradually becoming a universal, binding custom, and finally being included in a written code of laws. Second, we shall see how the law was interpreted in the years before Vatican II, how it was considered binding under pain of mortal sin, and then how this legalistic and moralistic approach changed dramatically in the 1960s and 1970s. Third, we will consider whether the Sunday Mass obligation is an adequate means anymore to promote the traditional observance of the Lord's Day, or whether urging this obligation today may do more harm than good.

From Local to Universal Law

There is no evidence in the early church of any positive legislation requiring the faithful's attendance at Sunday eucharist. The fact that the Christian community assembled each week on the Lord's Day is, however, indisputable. Over the course of time the church came to consider its assembling on Sunday for eucharist as normative and binding, but it remained an unwritten custom rather than a written law. The first time the Sunday Mass obligation was formally established in universal law was in the *Code of Canon Law* of 1917.

The earliest positive legislation on Sunday Mass observance came from local councils. The Council of Agde in 506 decreed that the faithful should not leave the Sunday eucharist before the blessing of the priest: "We enjoin by a special injunction that on the Lord's Day the laity shall be obliged to be present during the whole celebration of the Mass, so that the people do not presume to go out of church before the priest has given the Benediction."[3] In effect, this law did not establish a Sunday precept but insisted that the people stay for the entire Mass. Other local councils in the sixth century enacted similar legislation. Evidently, the problem of people leaving Mass early is not a new one.

From the seventh century on, numerous local councils treated matters related to Sunday Mass attendance. This body of legislation shows that, by this period, Christians in many local churches were obliged by law to assist at Sunday Mass unless they had a legitimate excuse to be absent. In many areas during the Middle Ages, the Sunday Mass obligation was supported by ecclesiastical or civil sanctions, including a variety of corporal punishments and fines. The laws were binding only in the localities for which they were enacted, not for the universal church.

From the thirteenth to fifteenth centuries, various local councils enacted legislation requiring that the Sunday Mass obligation be fulfilled only in one's parish church. These laws were prompted by the influence of the mendicant orders, which were attracting people away from the secular clergy on Sundays. Pope Sixtus IV (1471–1484) lent support to the secular clergy by forbidding the friars to tell the faithful that they were not bound to attend Mass on Sundays in their parishes.[4] These legislative attempts to solve the problem did not achieve the desired effect. Due to the continuing growth of the mendicant orders and the popularity of their preaching and pastoral care, these laws proved ineffective and were widely disregarded by the faithful. The Council of Trent did not enact binding legislation on this matter but simply decreed that local ordinaries should admonish the faithful to go to their parish church frequently, at least on Sundays and on principal feast days.[5]

From the end of the sixteenth to the middle of the eighteenth century, custom dictated that the Sunday Mass obligation could be fulfilled at any church, although it was debated whether the obligation could be satisfied in a private oratory by those who did not have an indult. For example, could servants fulfill their Sunday obligation in the private chapel of a noble family who had an indult, even if their service of the family was not required at that time? Pope Benedict XIV (1740–1758) settled the matter by excluding fulfillment of the obligation in a private oratory without an indult.[6] An exception was made for those attending Mass in the private oratory of a bishop when the bishop presided. This was basically the practice that came to be incorporated into the first *Code of Canon Law* of 1917.

Canon 1248 of the 1917 code prescribed the obligation of "hearing mass" on Sundays and holy days of obligation and also the obligation to abstain from servile work. Canon 1249 spelled out the Mass obligation in greater detail. It said that the obligation of hearing Mass is fulfilled by attending Mass celebrated in any Catholic rite, in the open air or in any church, public oratory or semipublic oratory. The precept could not be fulfilled in private oratories without an indult of the Apostolic See except in the private oratories of cardinals and bishops or in a private cemetery chapel.

Under Pain of Mortal Sin

The 1917 code bound all baptized persons who had the use of reason and who had completed their seventh year, including baptized non-Catholics. Even Protestants and Eastern non-Catholics, called heretics and schismatics, were legally bound to attend Mass each Sunday and holy day in a Catholic rite. Some authors believed that most non-Catholic Christians were morally excused from this obligation due to invincible ignorance of the law, while others believed that they committed mortal sin each Sunday and holy day by not attending a Catholic Mass.

Catholic moral theology and canon law in the period before Vatican II was characterized by an intense legalism and casuistry. Moral theology and canon law were closely allied disciplines, often taught in seminaries by the same professor. A deliberate violation of any church law was considered sinful, either mortally or venially, depending on the importance of the law that was broken. The Sunday Mass obligation, which was held to be a merely ecclesiastical and not a divine law, was nevertheless considered to be binding under pain of mortal sin.

From at least the time of Pope Innocent XI (1676–1689), it was common Catholic teaching that the customary Sunday Mass obligation was binding under pain of mortal sin. Authors differed over what parts of the Mass had to be heard to fulfill the obligation and how much of it could be missed before a mortal sin was committed. Most canonists and moralists agreed that the omission of one-third of the Mass sufficed to constitute grave matter, but they computed this variously according to what qualitative weight they gave the various parts of the Mass. The omission of short portions of the Mass, exclusive of the consecration, was considered a venial sin.

In actual practice, the faithful were taught they had to be present for the three "principal parts" of the Mass — the offertory, the consecration and communion. If they missed the Mass of the catechumens, that part prior to the offertory, they committed only venial sin. The authors also taught that the parts missed from a first Mass could be made up at a subsequent Mass, provided the consecration and communion were united at one and the same Mass. For example, a person arriving at the consecration of one Mass could avoid incurring a mortal sin by remaining until the preface of a second Mass. However, a person arriving shortly after the consecration would have to stay through the communion of the next Mass.

The precept of hearing Mass was said to be satisfied by moral bodily presence at Mass. The authors taught that this could be fulfilled, even if some persons were not bodily present in the church, if they were morally united to the congregation and present in the sacristy or in an adjoining room, courtyard or even adjacent house if they could follow the service through an open window. It was not considered sufficient to follow the Mass from a distance by means of a telescope, radio or television.

The authors taught that the subject of the law had to assist at the Mass with external attention. Even though a person were bodily present at Mass, the precept could not be fulfilled if one were in a state of complete intoxication; soundly asleep throughout a notable portion of the Mass; engaged in serious conversation during a notable part of the Mass; reading profane books which required intense concentration or even spiritual books for the exclusive sake of erudition, curiosity or information; writing letters or composing them; examining intently the statues or pictures or decorations in the church; concentrating intently on the music or singing; or spending a notable portion of the Mass examining the clothing of others.[7]

Canonists and moralists also noted examples of reasons that would excuse from the obligation, including illness, travel time to the church lasting more than an hour, circumstances which made a trip to church difficult, grave inconvenience, a pressing exercise of charity, unavoidable need to work or legitimate custom such as that which exempted widows in some areas from attending Mass during the time of their mourning.

A New Approach in Moral Theology

This intensely legalistic and moralistic interpretation of the law of the Sunday Mass obligation was characteristic of the approach to all ecclesiastical laws in the church's recent history before the Second Vatican Council. This same kind of legalism and casuistry could be seen in related matters, such as the observance of the law on days of fast and abstinence, Sunday rest, the fast before communion, the recitation of the divine office, and the like. However, by the 1960s a reaction against this kind of legalism began to grow strong as more and more scholars and pastors spoke out against it. They gave voice to a new way of thinking about canon law and moral theology. They frequently cited scriptural texts, especially from the gospels and from the writings of Saint Paul, arguing that the interior attitude of a person was more important than mere external observance of laws. They said, for example, that good Christians should want to come to Sunday Mass, observe the Sunday rest and do penance on Fridays and in Lent. They should not be compelled by external laws under the threat of mortal sin and eternal damnation.

Bernard Häring, in a book first published in German in 1960, downplayed the importance of attending Mass only in response to a law rather than in response to the Lord's invitation. He wrote that "much more is involved in the observance of the Sunday rest than a mere law of the church." The Sunday Mass is an invitation from Christ, he said, and we are being asked to participate in the heavenly worship. We fail to hear this invitation if we cling to the "bare minimum requirement of the law."[8]

Häring chastised those priests who, on the one hand, "stress with unrelenting repetition that there is a grave obligation to attend Mass on Sundays, but, on the other, do precious little to vitalize the eucharistic service." He said that "such priests incur greater guilt than the marginal Catholics who simply refuse to believe they have a Sunday obligation — or to be disturbed by it!" Häring was not trying to suggest that there is no Sunday obligation, nor that it did not bind under penalty of mortal sin. However, he spoke out strongly against a legalistic interpretation and enforcement of the Sunday precept: "That the Christian Sunday should descend to the level of mere fulfillment of a commandment to attend Mass is one of the saddest tragedies in the whole domain of spiritual life."[9] He believed that if priests celebrated liturgies that were worth attending, people would want to come to church whether or not there was a law obliging them to do so.

Charles Curran, writing in the mid-1960s, also took up the attack against an appeal to law to compel observance of the Sunday obligation. Although his discussion focused principally on the observance of the Sunday rest, his arguments often were also applicable to the Sunday Mass precept. Law and legislation, Curran wrote, cannot make Christianity, nor can mere external laws ever be the essence of Christianity. Christianity, he said, is essentially God's love for us manifested in creation, redemption and our destiny for eternal happiness in heaven. "Unfortunately, the fallacy of legalism has pervaded much of our thinking and our living. Who is a good Catholic? Everybody knows that a good Catholic is one who goes to Mass on Sunday and does not eat meat on Friday." Christ's criterion was quite different, Curran wrote, and he cited John 13:35: "By this will everyone know that you are my disciples if you have love for one another."

For Curran, "Christianity is primarily love, but not external law." Ecclesiastical legislation was never meant to be the source of Christian life, he said.

> The purely ecclesiastical laws exist for the harmony of the whole Christian community and to serve the individual Christian as guide markers — to point out only the minimal demands of the Christian law of love. . . . more and better legislation cannot be the ultimate answer to the problem of the Christian observance of Sunday. Over-insistence on such laws leads to the pharisaical formalism which Christ condemned so bitterly. We must

seek not the letter of the law but the spirit of the law. St. Paul reminds us that the "letter kills, but the spirit gives life" (2 Corinthians 3:6).[10]

Nowhere does Curran state in this discussion that missing Mass on Sundays is not a mortal sin. However, the role of external law in the life of the church is clearly downplayed, especially the legalistic interpretation of law that was so pervasive in the church during the time Curran was writing.

Throughout the 1960s and into the 1970s, the anti-legalistic theme was picked up by scholars and popularizers alike. In a book published in 1970, Christopher Kiesling, a theologian and popular writer at the time, reflected a view of the Sunday Mass obligation that was very close to that of Häring and Curran. Kiesling went even further, however, and explicitly stated that canon law should not impose any Sunday obligation, because it is ineffective. He said that the obligation should instead be placed on pastors to provide good worship experiences every Sunday for the Christian people. "Those who interpret the law should refrain from perverting it into a legal obligation binding on individual Christians."[11] He suggested that missing Mass might be a mortal sin in some situations, but not because it is against the law. He rejected the notion that sinfulness is involved merely because an ecclesiastical law is not observed. Rather, deliberate refusal or habitual neglect to participate in Sunday worship would be a serious sin because of the intrinsic value and importance of the community's worship for both itself and the individual.

The Sunday Obligation Today

In 1983 Pope John Paul II promulgated a thoroughly revised *Code of Canon Law* for Latin Catholics and in 1990 a first *Code of Canons of the Eastern Churches*. For Latin Catholics, the Sunday Mass obligation is retained in the church's revised legal code in canons 1247 and 1248. For Eastern Catholics, the obligation is found in canon 881 to attend the divine liturgy or, in accord with the laws and customs of the church, the divine praises (Liturgy of the Hours). The language of these laws speaks of "precept" and "binding obligation," although there no longer exists the former consensus that this obligation is binding under pain of mortal sin.

In what sense, therefore, can we still speak of a Sunday "obligation"? How is it binding? What are the consequences for not observing it? In the Middle Ages, the Mass obligation could be enforced by penalties, both ecclesiastical and civil. More recently, canon law has been enforced by threats of mortal sin and fear of hell. That option also is no longer viable and, indeed, is counterproductive. Contemporary adults cannot be compelled to go to church against their will. Consequently, if the Sunday obligation is going to have any meaning, it must be understood as a duty that springs from internal motivation, not from mere external authority. It is an obligation which the faithful themselves freely assume in response to their baptismal vocation and the consequent responsibilities they owe to the Christian community.

People rebel against authoritarian commands, but they often respond positively to challenges that draw on their own inner sense of right and duty. Rather than being commanded to do the minimal — merely to fulfill a legal obligation — Catholics should be challenged and inspired to do more. Catechesis must appeal to the faithful's basic religious sensibilities, their faith in God, their commitment to Christ and their loyalty to the church. An authoritarian approach based on external laws and fear of mortal sin will not work with contemporary Catholics. That approach is dead and cannot be revived.

An appeal to one's sense of religious duty, a sense which is felt interiorly and not imposed by law or by some remote ecclesiastical authority, will be the only compelling way to foster observance of the Sunday obligation. In order to accomplish this, much effort is still required to make individuals and parish communities realize existentially that their responsibility to go to church comes from their identity as being church. The Catholic people have not widely enough appreciated the ecclesiological recovery of Vatican II. They have not fully understood that they are church, that they are the people of God, the body of Christ. In too many parishes, the faithful still lack a sense of ownership of their church and of their dignity and equality as members of Christ's body. As a result, they also lack an appreciation of their duties owed to the church and of their Christian responsibilities to the world. They do not see how their presence at Sunday Mass helps to build up the body of Christ, and they fail to recognize that their absence hurts the body. Even those who attend church regularly often do so more for what they "get out of it" than for what they can contribute.

Christians celebrate eucharist on Sunday because that is the principal way they worship God collectively in response to Christ's mandate, "Do this as a memorial of me." The Sunday eucharistic celebration is the principal way the baptized signify who they are. By their presence and active participation at Sunday eucharist, they both constitute the church in its local manifestation and contribute to its upbuilding. The Sunday "obligation" is not primarily something individuals owe to God — God can be worshiped by private persons in other ways besides eucharist. Rather, the church's Sunday Mass obligation speaks of the relationship between the individual Christian and the Christian community. It is a binding obligation precisely because individuals have a duty to the other members of the community to whom they are committed by their baptism. By virtue of their baptism, they have a duty to build up the body of Christ, and the most fundamental way they contribute to this goal is by participating in the Sunday eucharist.

These profound truths cannot be appropriated merely by repeating a church precept. They must be internalized by the faithful through their experience of being church. This is most readily accomplished within the context of vital communities of faith whose liturgical celebrations, catechetical programs and outreach to the world constitute effective signs of what it is to be church. "Welcome back" programs to get people to return to church are doomed to fail if there is little to keep them coming afterward.

The Sunday Mass precept is no longer an effective means of maintaining a high level of Mass attendance. It has become a law without force, an obligation that only binds those who choose to be bound. Nor can the old understanding of the obligation be revived without further alienating people who are already overly suspicious of authority and law. If the Sunday Mass precept is to have an effect, it must become an internalized value, something that the people of God want to observe in virtue of their commitment to the church; it cannot be something they have to obey under threat of penalty or sin.

NOTES

[1]Mark Chaves and James C. Cavendish, "More Evidence on U.S. Catholic Church Attendance," *Journal for the Scientific Study of Religion* 33 (1994): 376 – 81.

[2]*American Catholics Since the Council: An Unauthorized Report* (Chicago: Thomas More, 1985): 71.

[3]Cited in William Hodgkins, *Sunday: Christian and Social Significance* (London: Independent Press, 1960): 26.

[4]John J. Guiniven, *The Precept of Hearing Mass* (Washington: Catholic University of America, 1942): 34.

[5]Sess. XXII, September, 1563, *Decretum de observandis et vitandis in celebratione missarum.*

[6]Guiniven, 38.

[7]Guiniven, 106 – 107.

[8]*The Law of Christ* (Westminster, Maryland: Newman, 1963): 313.

[9]Ibid., 313, 311.

[10]*Christian Morality Today: The Renewal of Moral Theology* (Notre Dame: Fides, 1966): 109 –110.

[11]*The Future of the Christian Sunday* (New York: Sheed and Ward, 1970): 33.

Daily Mass: Law and Spirituality

When the eucharist is celebrated by the same group of people every day over a long period, it is not unusual for some members of the community occasionally to have bad experiences with this regimen. On the one hand, a daily rite that is nearly always the same can result in boredom for people who like variety and change. On the other hand, in communities where novelty and creativity in the liturgy is a conscious aim, the constant need for planning new celebrations every day can lead to liturgical exhaustion on the part of presiders, ministers of music and others involved in liturgical leadership.

This essay is primarily directed to those who are obliged by law or by the requirements of their profession to participate in the eucharist every day: clergy, religious, seminarians and lay liturgical ministers like musicians and cantors. Secondarily, it is directed to other persons who freely commit themselves, on a regular or periodic basis, to attending weekday Mass. The constitutions of many religious institutes and the policies of seminaries and formation programs require attendance at daily Mass; also, priests and other liturgical ministers in parishes frequently must be at Mass nearly every day one or more times as part of their job, and so it is also a duty for them, even if not a duty imposed by law. However, a growing number of persons in this group have not acquired, or have lost over time, a spirituality centered on daily eucharistic celebration. For some this is due to their own vision of the nature and purpose of the eucharist, which is based on the primacy of the Sunday assembly. Liturgist John Baldovin, for example, has critiqued the routine practice of daily Mass in parishes from historical, theological and pastoral perspectives.[1]

Baldovin's solution to the problems he raises is to celebrate the eucharist on weekdays only on special occasions such as important feasts, weddings, ordinations and other celebrations. But that is not a realistic solution, and for many Catholics it is not a desirable one. There is a small but significant body of people — laity, religious and clergy — for whom daily Mass is the high point of their daily prayer and their personal spirituality. What pastor would want to withdraw from them a spiritual practice that the popes of the twentieth century have regularly urged as the ideal? Rather than stopping the centuries-old practice of daily eucharist, I suggest instead that we reflect on what daily Mass means to people, what their "spirituality of daily Mass" might be and whether the weekday Mass as celebrated in parish or community is responding to these various spiritualities.

It may be helpful for everyone who attends daily Mass, whether by desire or obligation, to recognize the different values and motivations of others. One way to come at this is to see these different values and attitudes as different spiritualities, each of which, in a certain sense, is reflected in church law. A case can be made that there are three distinct spiritualities of daily Mass implicit in twentieth century canon law, and that these three different approaches also characterize the liturgical style preferences of those who regularly attend weekday Mass.

These three approaches might be called by shorthand names: the first is "duty"; the second is "another Sunday"; the third is "personal devotion." The experience of daily Mass as a duty is most likely to be that of liturgical ministers, clergy, seminarians, religious and members of secular institutes and societies of apostolic life who generally are expected to attend Mass daily or may even be bound to do so by particular laws or job expectations. The second approach, another Sunday, is most likely also to be found in this group of the faithful; others who have this approach tend not to attend weekday Mass on a regular basis. The third spirituality, that of "personal devotion," exists among all groups of the faithful and is proportionately strongest among Catholics who willingly and without a sense of obligation attend daily Mass over the span of many years. Finally, it must be noted that it is common for the same individual to share two or even all three of the spiritualities in varying degrees.

Duty Spirituality

One spirituality of daily eucharist, that of "duty," was reflected in the 1917 *Code of Canon Law* in its laws on the spiritual duties of seminarians, religious and priests. Canon 595 of the former code listed a number of spiritual duties of religious whose observance the superior was to enforce. Among these duties, superiors were to see that religious in their charge attended Mass every day unless they were legitimately impeded from doing so. Likewise, canon 1367 listed various spiritual duties of seminarians. Among these, the bishop was to see that they participated in the sacrifice of the Mass every day. The former law was directed not to individual religious and seminarians but to their superiors. The bishop was required to see that seminarians went to daily Mass; religious superiors were required to see that their subjects did the same. Weekday Mass was one of the daily duties of religious life and the seminary regimen together with other forms of prayer and spiritual exercises, including for many the recitation of the Divine Office. Priests were legally obliged to celebrate Mass several times a year; the bishop or clerical religious superior was obliged to see that their priests celebrated Mass at least on all Sundays and holy days of obligation. They were, of course, also legally obliged to pray all the hours of the Divine Office every day (1917 CIC, canons 805, 135).

Under the former law, participation in daily Mass was a duty of religious and seminarians that religious superiors and bishops were charged with enforcing. Priests were obliged to celebrate Mass only several times a year. In point of fact, however, most priests were required to celebrate Mass daily to satisfy the canonical obligation to apply the fruits of the Mass for the special intentions for which stipends had been accepted. Before the liturgical reforms, scarcely anyone thought the weekday Mass had to be meaningful; it was only considered necessary to celebrate it rubrically correct. The Mass was said to have objective value; it gave grace no matter how well or how poorly it was celebrated. Weekday Mass was typically a "low Mass," quickly read in Latin by a priest in dialogue with a server. Clerical religious celebrated a private Mass at a side altar or they attended the conventual Mass in common; other members of the faithful frequently prayed their rosaries or followed along with hand missals as the priest enacted the unbloody sacrifice of the cross in the sanctuary. There was no thought of variation or innovation. The ideal was ritual uniformity and rubrical exactitude. Mass was "said" or "read," not "celebrated."

Even today there are many people whose routine participation in the Mass is principally motivated by a sense of duty. Those who see the Mass primarily as a duty are more likely to want a liturgical style that is fairly uniform each day unless it is a major feast, when they will enjoy greater solemnity. Important values for such people are regularity and punctuality. They want the Mass to begin on time and to finish before the next scheduled event in their daily schedule.

The more that "duty" is one's motivation for attendance at daily Mass, the less likely it is that one will be interested in contributing to meaningful liturgies for others in the community. When people are motivated to attend Mass merely out of a sense of duty to external law, their preparation for and participation in the liturgy often suffer. Frequently the chief objective is to get it finished quickly so that the obligation is fulfilled.

On the other hand, there are positive values in the duty approach that optimally ought to be part of the spirituality of every Christian. Although many today are strongly opposed to a spiritual discipline based on external law, the values underlying the law should not be discounted. The eucharist is the principal liturgical celebration of the Christian life. When religious constitutions or seminary regulations require members' participation in the eucharist every day, the law is calling on religious and seminarians to make the church's principal act of worship also a principal act of this local community so that each member of the community may draw spiritual nourishment from God's word and from the sacrificial meal, and so that the symbolic memorializing of Christ's paschal mystery can help build up this community of faith every day. Such a sense of duty arises not from some external norm of law, whether of canon law or constitutions, but rather from a recognition of the important values underlying the law.

Another Sunday Spirituality

Canon law, in effect, says very little about weekday Mass. Nowhere in the code are the faithful in general encouraged, much less required, to attend daily Mass. There is, of course, a law requiring attendance at Mass on Sundays and holy days of obligation (canon 1247). But nothing is said in the law about attending Mass on weekdays except in the case of seminarians, clergy and members of religious and secular institutes who are encouraged to participate in the eucharist daily.

In addition to the *Code of Canon Law,* another major body of canon law is the law contained in the liturgical books. The liturgical laws governing the eucharist have as their frame of reference the Sunday Mass, not the weekday Mass. They are written for the most part with the Sunday assembly in mind — the gathered *ecclesia* in the public setting of parish or cathedral. Many clergy, religious and laity who have studied liturgy in courses or workshops have been schooled in the theology of Sunday and the centrality of the eucharistic celebration on the Lord's Day. Some have been trained in liturgical music, homiletics and other skills. This academic and pastoral formation focuses mainly on the Sunday liturgy. It is not surprising, then, that the approach of many toward weekday eucharist is that of "another Sunday." They assume, often without thinking, that the liturgical requirements of Sunday are equally applicable to weekdays. They employ on weekdays a Sunday style of celebration.

Those who see daily Mass as another Sunday want a celebration with as much music as they can muster; they expect well-prepared, formal homilies; and in general they adopt a ritual style associated with large-group liturgies on Sundays and feast days. The chief problem with this approach to weekday Mass is the demand it makes on liturgical planners and ministers and on the assembly itself. It is particularly demanding when the community has only a small number of presiders and liturgical musicians. It takes much time to construct a good homily, and few ministers have the energy or ability to do this every day. Likewise, few communities have either the resources or the desire for a eucharist with complete musical participation every day. Over time, the "another Sunday" approach leads to liturgical burnout. Ironically, it diminishes enthusiasm for the central liturgical celebration of the week — that of the Sunday eucharist — which can become for them just one more daily liturgy to prepare and get through, just another Mass like every other one.

The Sunday eucharist in the public assembly is the paradigm for all eucharistic celebrations, and that is why the liturgical laws concentrate on it. While the law looks to Sunday Mass as the type or model for all eucharistic celebrations, it is necessary that this type be adapted for other, small-group liturgies on weekdays. Liturgical planners and ministers must be guided by the *principle of progressive solemnity.* Sundays and major feast days should be celebrated with full solemnity — with penitential rite or sprinkling with holy water; Gloria and Creed; preparation of the gifts; processions; sung acclamations, hymns and other forms of music; a well-prepared homily based on the scripture readings or other texts of the Mass; and other verbal and ritual elements that make for festive liturgical celebration.

On other days, ritual options should be omitted or reduced in number so that the Sunday liturgy is not supplanted by greater solemnity during the week. On an ordinary weekday when no major feast is being celebrated, it suffices to sing the principal acclamations with or without accompaniment; that is, the responsorial psalm (if a cantor is present), the gospel acclamation, sanctus, memorial acclamation and Amen. To this could be added a commmunion song and perhaps a few other chants or songs, such as the Our Father or Lamb of God, in accord with the worshiping community's customs and wishes. The homily might be a brief reflection, or it could be replaced with a meditative pause to allow God's word to penetrate into the hearts of the hearers. The spirit of the weekday liturgy should be that of noble simplicity and brevity, true to the tradition of the Roman rite. Toward this end, it would be pastorally beneficial to have an adapted rite of Mass for weekdays, omitting nonessential elements such as the penitential and offertory rites and simplifying the order of Mass in other ways.[2]

On the positive side, those who are steeped in a liturgical spirituality with a focus on Sunday frequently have a great love for the liturgy and often are gifted with liturgical talents — musical, artistic and homiletic — that produce effective celebration. Such persons contribute to the community's weekday assembling for eucharist in many ways and help to make it a more fruitful experience for all. The gifts and talents of such persons will be most appreciated when they observe the principle of progressive solemnity and do not overwhelm the weekday assembly with "too much of a good thing" every day.

Personal Devotion Spirituality

The third spirituality underlying the law on daily eucharist is that of "personal devotion." This was the spirituality behind the exhortations of popes and pastors to attend Mass and receive communion daily. This spirituality is also reflected in the 1983 *Code of Canon Law,* at least in the case of seminarians, clergy and members of religious and secular institutes who are exhorted to celebrate or attend Mass daily (canons 246, 276, 904, 663, 719). Unlike the Liturgy of the Hours, which clergy are bound by law to celebrate daily, participation in the weekday eucharist is a recommendation, not an obligation. As for religious and seminarians, no longer is there an obligation placed on superiors and bishops to see that individual religious and seminarians attend. The law now addresses individuals directly, not their superiors. The new code speaks not in the language of duty and obligation but in the language of recommendation, exhortation and encouragement. The canon on the spiritual duties of seminarians is a good example of this use of hortatory rather than strongly preceptive language:

> The celebration of the most holy eucharist is to be the center of the entire life of the seminary so that the students, sharing the very love of Christ, may daily draw from this richest of all sources the strength of spirit needed for their apostolic work and their spiritual life (canon 246, §1).

The law views daily Mass as the spiritual ideal, but it leaves it up to the individual to strive to attain this ideal without imposing any direct obligations on superiors and bishops to enforce this practice.

As in the former code, weekday Mass is treated in the new code along with other spiritual and liturgical practices, including Liturgy of the Hours, devotions to the Blessed Virgin Mary, meditation, the sacrament of penance and an annual retreat. It is clear that the legislator considers daily Mass part of the spiritual regimen of the church's "professionals" to help them develop a sound personal spirituality and to grow in holiness. However, the language of the code is new — that of exhortation rather than strict obligation.

While this approach is certainly to be preferred over the imposition of a legal obligation to attend daily Mass, it should be remembered that some are obliged to attend Mass every day by particular law. This is especially true of many religious institutes and most seminaries. If the personal devotion approach is not applied in the right spirit by these groups, it can undermine the ecclesial value of daily Mass, which is one of the values that underlies the law. For religious and seminarians, daily Mass celebrated in common is a chief way that the religious community's or seminary's communal life is built up and nourished. It is not simply a way of developing one's private spirituality.

This is also an issue for parish clergy. In a parish, if the pastor or another priest sees daily Mass only in terms of personal devotion, a devotionalized approach to presiding can result that may witness well to the priest's own piety but may do little to build up an authentic community of faith for all those present.

Daily eucharist is not, in fact, a necessary requirement for personal holiness, not even, as the code might seem to imply, for clergy, seminarians and religious. There are many ways a person can grow spiritually. Indeed, if daily community eucharist were intended only for personal spiritual growth, then seminarians and religious who may be obliged by laws or policies to attend daily Mass could rightly claim that they personally do not need this discipline. They could correctly assert, as they sometimes do, that they would benefit more by working in the apostolate or by praying to God in the quiet of their own rooms. But experience shows that when such individualistic spiritualities predominate, the common life of the religious house or seminary often weakens and the communal spirit and morale of its members suffer.

The duty approach of the old law, and indeed of current law embodied in religious constitutions and seminary regulations, can help to balance a one-sided emphasis on attending daily Mass solely for reasons of personal spiritual growth or devotion. Religious, seminarians and other groups who are committed to celebrating daily Mass as a community need to recover for themselves a notion of the Mass that is not unlike that of the Liturgy of the Hours — a *divinum officium,* a divine office, a religious duty. For centuries this has been modelled by religious institutes who daily celebrate in common the Liturgy of the Hours as well as the eucharist. For them, daily Mass is one of the regular duties of religious life together with other forms of prayer and spiritual exercises, especially morning and evening prayer. The Mass is part of their daily office, their daily duty. It is one of the hours of the day the community keeps in prayer.

This does not imply a return to a view of daily Mass as an external requirement imposed by the law and enforced by a superior. Rather, what is needed is an internally appropriated sense of duty. With an internalized sense of duty, individuals do not necessarily go to daily Mass because they find it the most meaningful prayer for them personally. Rather, they go because they are committed to this community and want to help build it up by their presence and active participation at one of the community's daily acts. This also applies to parish priests and liturgical ministers for whom daily Mass may not be a strong spiritual value but whose presence and leadership is required or expected by parishioners who strongly value attendance at Mass every day.

Complementarity of the Models

Canon law in the twentieth century implies three different spiritualities of daily Mass, and these different approaches are often represented by various individuals in the same worshiping community. Whether this be in a seminary or religious community, a parish or other community, there are individuals who themselves have different spiritualities of and attitudes toward daily Mass. Each of the three spiritualities has something positive to contribute.

Those who approach the liturgy as a daily duty can model for everyone a sense of fidelity to prayer and loyalty to parish or community. They contribute to the liturgy and to the upbuilding of the local community by their steady presence at the eucharist day in and day out. They witness to the daily struggle of each Christian who is called by baptism to grow in fidelity to the gospel vocation of discipleship and holiness of life.

Those who approach the eucharist from the model of the Sunday liturgy can remind all in the community of the dignity and importance of every eucharistic celebration. The eucharist is not just another duty in one's daily horarium, nor is it simply a means for individuals to receive communion, get grace and grow spiritually. It is an ecclesial act, the principal ritual act of the church, which celebrates the dying and rising of the Lord. Liturgical ministers who like festivity at liturgy every day can be of service to all by enlivening the eucharist with their homiletic, musical or artistic talents while keeping in mind the principle of progressive solemnity.

Those, finally, who look to daily Mass primarily as a source of spiritual strength and refreshment and as an expression of personal devotion can contribute to the liturgy by the witness of their own sincerity and piety. Their words, gestures and attitudes at liturgy bespeak the sacredness of the event and thus help to make it a more meaningful and more deeply spiritual experience for all.

Each of the three different spiritualities gives rise to different attitudes toward and different ways of celebrating weekday Mass. When one spirituality dominates to the detriment of the other two, the pastoral benefit of the liturgy is diminished and some members of the community may be alienated. When the three are held in balance, the daily eucharist has a wider appeal and effectiveness.

Each parish and local community that has committed itself to celebrate eucharist on weekdays needs to find a style of celebration or a variety of styles that attempt to meet the spiritualities of the members. This may seem a daunting task given the variety of personalities and attitudes, but it can be accomplished. With sensitivity to others, open dialogue and goodwill, the weekday assemblies can develop their own style of celebration that will help all members experience the eucharistic liturgy more fully as the source and summit of the Christian life.

NOTES

[1]"Reflections on the Frequency of Eucharistic Celebration," *Worship* 61 (1987): 2–15. The summary of his views here tries to capture his major points, even using his own words in many cases.

[2]See the suggestions of Aelred Tegels, "Chronicle," *Worship* 59 (1985): 154–55.

The Liturgy of the Hours in Parishes

In the early church the celebration of the eucharist each day was not known; the rule was "the Lord's supper on the Lord's day."[1] On weekdays, the Christian community assembled in the cathedral or parish church to sing praise and thanks to God at morning and evening prayer. Current liturgical law, reflecting a principal aim of the liturgical movement, strongly encourages the communal celebration of the Liturgy of the Hours in parishes. This is not to suggest that the Liturgy of the Hours is to replace daily Mass, unless the eucharist has already disappeared due to the lack of a pastor. But it does indicate that the daily celebration of the hours in parishes enjoys as strong a place in Catholic tradition as does daily eucharist.

> Our churches today are used for scarcely anything apart from the celebration of Mass. . . . Certainly, the Mass already presents us with a most important element of divine praise and thanksgiving.

> However, one may reasonably ask whether Christians who never practice divine praise for its own sake, and who do not come to church except [for the Mass], have a true idea of what the eucharist is.

This critique of parish worship, written by liturgical scholar A. M. Roguet in 1971 at the time the reformed Liturgy of the Hours was introduced,[2] regrettably still holds true today in most parishes. Why have the goals of the liturgical reform been thoroughly implemented in terms of the eucharistic liturgy but woefully neglected in respect to the Liturgy of the Hours? Could part of the reason be that many still view the Liturgy of the Hours as a clerical obligation and not as a celebration of the whole church?

This essay proposes to shed some light on these questions, especially from the perspective of liturgical law, and to make concrete suggestions for the regular celebration of morning and/or evening prayer in every parish. The first part will briefly summarize the history of popular participation in the Liturgy of the Hours. The second part will offer some ideas for the implementation of the Liturgy of the Hours in parishes, and the third part will show that although the clerical obligation to recite the Liturgy of the Hours still exists in the law, the law taken as a whole actually favors communal celebration with the laity.

History

The daily, public liturgical celebrations of the early church were morning and evening prayer, which began as early as the third century and were flourishing nearly everywhere by the middle of the fourth century. Eusebius, bishop of Caesarea in Palestine in the early part of the fourth century, noted that throughout the Christian world, morning and evening prayer were celebrated publicly and daily.[3] The public celebrations of morning and evening prayer, commonly known today as the "cathedral office," were well attended by the faithful. These liturgies "were indeed gatherings of the people: the faithful sang 'morning psalms' and 'evening psalms' which did not vary and which they knew by heart; to these were added, especially in the morning, biblical and even non-biblical canticles; in some churches there was a sermon almost every day."[4]

Morning prayer was the prayer of Christians as they began their day. As they rose to the life of a new day, they recalled each morning the resurrection of Christ. They consecrated their day to God through this prayer of praise and thanksgiving. Evening prayer was sung at the hour when people had finished their work and the light of day was dying. In many places the lighting of lamps or candles, the *lucernarium,* was an impressive part of the liturgy. The assembly praised God and gave thanks for the benefits they had received during the day. As their morning prayer at the time of the rising sun had called to mind the resurrection of the Son of God, their evening prayer at the dying of the day recalled his passion and death. Each day, through the liturgical hours kept in the morning and evening, the Christian community shared anew in Christ's paschal mysteries.

In the Middle Ages participation by the people in the public celebration of the Liturgy of the Hours declined and nearly ceased. They no longer understood Latin, and the hours became more elaborate and variable, requiring costly manuscripts. The Liturgy of the Hours became more and more the preserve of monks and clerics, the church's "professional class" who were educated in Latin and had the time to pray the various hours—not only morning and evening prayer (lauds and vespers) but also prime, terce, sext, none, compline and matins. The Liturgy of the Hours became known as *divinum officium,* the divine office, which means a spiritual duty or obligation. Although religious continued to celebrate the hours in common, the secular clergy read the office privately from smaller books, called "breviaries." By the High Middle Ages many clergy understood that the divine office was their duty and right and theirs alone; they were not aware of the laity's active participation at the Liturgy of the Hours in earlier centuries.[5] However, lay participation in the Liturgy of the Hours never died out entirely. Even into the twentieth century, Sunday vespers survived in parishes, and attendance was sometimes quite large even though active participation was reduced to the singing of a few hymns while the clergy and choir sang the rest of it.

The Second Vatican Council sought to restore the communal dimension of all liturgical celebrations: "Liturgical services are not private functions but are celebrations of the church . . . and they pertain to the whole body of the church" (SC, 26). Regarding the Liturgy of the Hours, the *Constitution on the Sacred Liturgy* called upon clerics, especially priests who live together or who assemble for any purpose, to pray at least some part of the divine office in common (SC, 99). Vatican II also exhorted those involved in pastoral ministry to see to it that the principal hours, especially evening prayer, are celebrated communally in churches on Sundays and on major feasts, and it encouraged clergy to celebrate the hours together with the laity (SC, 100).

The *General Instruction of the Liturgy of the Hours,* 33 is most emphatic on the desirability of communal celebration with the laity: "Celebration in common shows more clearly the ecclesial nature of the Liturgy of the Hours. It fosters the active participation of all, according to their individual role, through acclamations, dialogues, alternating psalmody and the like." Communal celebration, therefore, "is to be preferred to individual and quasi-private celebration."

Pastoral Suggestions

Despite the clear teachings of the church, communal celebration of the Liturgy of the Hours in parishes remains for the most part an unrealized dream. For busy parish priests, introducing the faithful to the celebration of the Liturgy of the Hours has not been a priority. All too frequently, parish schedules are already burdened by numerous Masses and other liturgical and devotional celebrations. Also, the Liturgy of the Hours as given in the breviary is at times a complicated form of prayer, especially on feasts and during special seasons. It would require practice and effort to enable the laity to pray it correctly at all times.

These difficulties are understandable, but none of it is insurmountable. For communal celebration to succeed in parishes, it will often be necessary to adapt the Liturgy of the Hours to a simple, standard format (GILH, 246–252). Not everyone present needs to have the complete book of hours. It would be sufficient for them to have a book of the psalms and canticles or a pamphlet containing several exemplars of morning or evening prayer that could be used over and over. A number of Catholic publishers have books and pamphlets with settings for the Liturgy of the Hours suitable for parish celebration.[6] The hymn could be taken from the parish hymnal. Only the presider and other available ministers, such as the reader and cantor, would need books for the proper parts.

When a cleric participates in a celebration adapted for the laity, he need not repeat the hour to fulfill his obligation (GILH, 242). The value of celebrating the hours with others communally is greater than that of praying them exactly as they appear in the liturgical books.

Success in introducing communal celebrations of the hours also depends on scheduling. Some parishes have resurrected the church's longstanding tradition of solemn Sunday vespers. A downtown parish would more likely attract people during the week after the workday. Another opportune time for the Liturgy of the Hours is morning prayer on Holy Thursday, Good Friday and Holy Saturday, when the eucharist cannot be celebrated. Morning prayer easily fills a void on these days for those parishioners who are accustomed to attending daily morning Mass. Morning and/or evening prayer could be celebrated every day during Lent and possibly also during the Easter season. The faithful are more likely during Lent to respond to an invitation to come for additional prayer in church than they are at any other time of the year, and the habits acquired during Lent might over time lead to a yearning for the hours during the Easter season as well and ultimately throughout the entire year.

In some places a deacon, a religious or a lay person leads morning prayer instead of eucharist when the pastor is away. This is a routine practice in some priestless parishes. Scholars and pastoral liturgists have raised serious objections to the frequent resort to communion services on Sundays,[7] but the practice has some historical warrant on weekdays. Even in places where a communion service has already been introduced on Sundays, the Liturgy of the Hours can be celebrated in conjunction with it. As an option, the service may still include the lectionary readings of the day instead of the brief reading from morning or evening prayer.

In parishes that routinely have more than one daily Mass, it may be possible to replace one Mass with morning prayer led by a priest, deacon or lay presider. Morning prayer might also be celebrated in church before one of the Masses each day. Experience shows that parishioners who come regularly for daily Mass are those who are most receptive to morning prayer as well. In some places, the introduction of the Liturgy of the Hours might be more successful in the evening than in the morning, with evening prayer on one or more weekdays in addition to vespers on Sundays.

The use of the word "successful" here is not intended to mean that the Liturgy of the Hours will have wide popular appeal any more than does weekday Mass. The gatherings for communal celebration of the hours in most places are usually quite small except on occasions of special solemnity. "Success" in this matter should not depend on the numbers in attendance. Even two or three gathered in Christ's name is ecclesially significant, because they gather precisely as *church* to sanctify the day and their activities, to give praise to God and to make intercession for the needs of the world.

The Liturgy of the Hours, whether prayed by clergy, religious or laity, is an official liturgical celebration carried out in the name of the church (canon 834, §2; GILH, 13–16). Therefore any attempt to foster the communal celebration of the Liturgy of the Hours in a parish, no matter how small the response, must be considered successful by comparison to the total neglect of this liturgical rite in most parishes.

The Clerical Obligation

From the Middle Ages until the Second Vatican Council, the celebration of the Liturgy of the Hours had been the preserve of the clergy, both secular and religious. It was even at times seen as an exclusively clerical prerogative. Unfortunately, the idea still persists that the Liturgy of the Hours is an arcane rite reserved for clergy and religious rather than a liturgical celebration of the whole church. As long as the Liturgy of the Hours continues to be regarded in this way, lay people are not going to have any interest in it. As long as pastors continue to view the Divine Office as their own particular duty, or burden, then they will easily overlook its role as a central part of the church's daily worship that is meant to be a meaningful and valuable celebration available to all.

With the reform of the Liturgy of the Hours, the obligation of clerics to recite the Divine Office is no longer understood in the intensely legalistic and moralistic way that characterized the pre–Vatican II approach. In the preconciliar period, canon law was closely wedded with moral theology. Clerics in major orders were personally obliged to recite the entire office each day, and the omission of any part of the office was considered a mortal sin.

Many priests experienced the Divine Office as more of a burden than a liturgical celebration that was a meaningful part of their prayer life. Like the laity, they frequently turned to non-liturgical practices and devotions to meet their real spiritual needs while the office became a rote, mechanical duty. To make this duty easier to fulfill, it was not required that the hours be prayed at their proper times. The obligation could be satisfied as long as all the canonical hours were said at any time within the course of the 24 hours of the day.

The clerical obligation to pray the Divine Office each day still exists in canon law. However, the observance of the requirement today is understood in a new way in accord with the spirit of the liturgical renewal. The *General Instruction of the Liturgy of the Hours* refers to the "mandate" given by the church to its clergy to pray the Liturgy of the Hours daily. However, it speaks of this mandate only after first focusing on the action of the whole church as it continues the prayer of Christ. The Liturgy of the Hours is the prayer of all God's people, the church, by which the times of day and night and all human life are sanctified (GILH, 10–17). All who take part in this prayer, including the laity, fulfill the duty *(officium)* of the church (SC, 85; GILH, 15).

Canon 1173 of the *Code of Canon Law* presents a brief but rich theology of this prayer: "In celebrating the Liturgy of the Hours, the church fulfills the priestly function of Christ; it hears God speaking to his people, memorializes the mystery of salvation, gives praise to God in song and prayer without interruption, and intercedes for the salvation of the whole world."[8] Celebrating the paschal mysteries, praising God in prayer and song, keeping the whole day holy — these worthy deeds are not clerical prerogatives but are said to belong to the whole church. The code says that all the faithful "are earnestly invited to participate in the Liturgy of the Hours inasmuch as it is the action of the church" (canon 1174, §2).

When the mandate to pray the Liturgy of the Hours is received by clergy at their ordination, they take on the obligation to pray this official liturgy daily *in the name of the whole church.* Through this mandate the whole church is assured that the hours of the day are being sanctified without ceasing. Laity, too, who pray the Liturgy of the Hours do so "in the name of the whole body of Christ, in fact in the person of Christ himself" (GILH, 108).

Priests (bishops and presbyters) and transitional deacons are bound to pray the Divine Office by virtue of their ordination (canon 276, §2, 3°). The obligation begins on the day they are ordained deacons, as do other clerical obligations such as celibacy and obedience. Also, lay members of institutes of consecrated life and societies of apostolic life may be bound by their constitutions to parts of the Liturgy of the Hours (canon 1174, §1), especially morning and evening prayer. Permanent deacons are not bound to the Liturgy of the Hours by the universal law but are to follow the prescripts of the bishops' conference of their nation. In the United States, permanent deacons are strongly encouraged to say morning and evening prayer and "should not hold themselves lightly excused" from praying these hours daily.[9]

The liturgical law specifies what is entailed by the clerical mandate to recite the Liturgy of the Hours. The *General Instruction of the Liturgy of the Hours,* 29 says that priests and transitional deacons "should recite the full sequence of the hours each day, as far as possible at the appropriate times." The law uses the subjunctive mood. It has the quality of an exhortation, translated as "should" in English, not that of a strong command, as would be indicated with "must." The use of this jussive subjunctive suggests that the recitation of the complete office each day is the ideal to which clergy should aspire. However, it does not follow that a cleric commits mortal sin if he fails to attain this ideal.

A Hierarchy of Hours

The *General Instruction of the Liturgy of the Hours,* 29 continues its treatment of the clerical mandate to pray the office by differentiating a "hierarchy" of the hours. The obligation binds more strongly for the more important hours, less strongly for the others. The principal hours are morning and evening prayer, called the "hinges" of the Liturgy of the Hours. These hours are not to be omitted "except for a serious reason."

The Bishops' Committee on the Liturgy of the United States episcopal conference understands this to mean that omission of morning and evening prayer by clergy should be exceptional. However, the BCL says that the individual priest or deacon has the necessary discretion to judge the gravity of the cause; it also warns against the danger of self-deception on this point.[10] A legalistic and moralistic approach is avoided. Freedom of conscience and maturity of faith are respected.

Second place in the hierarchy of hours is given to the office of readings, formerly called matins. Paragraph 29 of the GILH says that clergy "should faithfully recite the office of readings, which is above all a liturgical celebration of the word of God. In this way they fulfill daily a duty that is particularly their own, that is, of receiving the word of God into their lives so that they may become more perfect as disciples of the Lord and experience more deeply the unfathomable riches of Christ."

With its lengthy readings, this hour is better suited for private prayer and spiritual reading than for common celebration. Moreover, it can be prayed at any time during the day or at any time after evening prayer of the previous day. Regarding the obligation attached to this hour, the BCL notes that "a lesser reason excuses from its observance than the serious reason mentioned in the case of the two chief hours, morning and evening prayer."

In the third rank of the hierarchy are the lesser hours of daytime prayer and night prayer. "In order to sanctify the whole day more perfectly," GILH, 29 states that clergy "will have also at heart the recitation of the daytime hour and night prayer, to round off the whole 'work of God' and to commend themselves to God before retiring." The obligation entails the praying of one of the daytime hours — either midmorning prayer, midday prayer or midafternoon prayer (GILH, 77) — and night prayer, also called compline. Since these are the least important of the hours, minor reasons excuse from their observance.

The Proper Time

A major aim of the Second Vatican Council relative to the reform of the Liturgy of the Hours was to restore the celebration of the hours to the proper times of day (SC, 89, 94). This objective is reflected in both the *Code of Canon Law* (canon 1175) and in liturgical law (GILH, 11, 29). Morning prayer is to be prayed in the morning; evening prayer is to be prayed in the evening.

In the rigoristic, preconciliar practice, the cleric who did not have an opportunity to recite a certain canonical hour at the prescribed time was required to fulfill it at some other time that day. Now if a cleric misses a certain hour of the office, only the most rigid interpretation of the current law would require that he should make it up at a different time that day. Although this rigoristic view is not defective from a strictly literal reading of the law, it fails to capture the new spirit behind the law but harkens back to the mentality that characterized the preconciliar approach.

The new approach to the observance of the law ought not result in laxity in the celebration of the hours. In fact, if the spirit of the liturgical reform is really taken to heart, the new liturgical law is far more challenging than the old. It demands, firstly, that clergy and others who pray the Liturgy of the Hours do so with greater attention and devotion and that they improve their understanding of the liturgy and the Bible, especially the psalms (SC, 90; GILH, 19). It demands, secondly, that the hours be prayed at their proper times and celebrated communally whenever this is possible.

The preconciliar approach to the canonical obligation to pray the Liturgy of the Hours was, in a real sense, much less demanding on the priest than the requirements and ideals expressed in the current law. Formerly, the cleric in a major order could rather easily satisfy his obligation in private at a time of his own convenience. Now, much more is expected of those who truly want to pray the Liturgy of the Hours according to the mind of the church. Gone are the threats of mortal sin and eternal damnation for the omission of a canonical hour. In its place is the challenge to pray communally, to include the laity in the celebration as much as possible, to pray at the proper times and to pray with faith and devotion.

Conclusion

The Liturgy of the Hours is the traditional daily liturgical prayer of the church, a prayer of praise and thanksgiving celebrated each day at various hours but most importantly in the morning and evening. It is a prayer of the whole church — of clergy, religious and laity. If the faithful realistically are ever going to be receptive to the Liturgy of the Hours, they must be educated about its meaning and importance and be guided in its celebration. This requires the cooperation of parish leadership. As the BCL noted: "It is both the responsibility and opportunity for priests, who are the leaders of the Christian community, to assemble the praying people of God and join with them in the church's prayer."[11] The pastor, as leader of the parish and its worship, principally has this duty. But if the pastor or another parish priest is unable or unwilling to make this effort, it may fall to deacons, lay parish ministers or parishioners themselves to assume the responsibility to see that their parish has the opportunity to join with the whole church in sanctifying each day through the celebration of the Liturgy of the Hours.

NOTES

[1]Nathan Mitchell, *Cult and Controversy: The Worship of the Eucharist Outside Mass* (New York: Pueblo, 1982): 15.

[2]*The Liturgy of the Hours: The General Instruction with Commentary* (Collegeville: Liturgical Press, 1971): 77.

[3]*Commentary on Psalm 64,* cited in Stanislaus Campbell, "Liturgy of the Hours," NDSW, 563. See also Josef A. Jungmann, *The Early Liturgy to the Time of Gregory the Great* (University of Notre Dame, 1959): 106.

[4]Aimé Georges Martimort, "The Liturgy of the Hours," in Irénée H. Dalmais, Pierre Jounel, and A.M. Martimort, *The Church at Prayer 4: The Liturgy and Time* (Collegeville: Liturgical Press, 1986): 171–72.

[5]During the debates on communion under both kinds at the Council of Constance in 1415, Andrew of Brod argued that if lay people were permitted to drink from the chalice at Mass they would then want to take on other clerical prerogatives, including taking an active part in the Mass, reading the scriptures, "and perhaps even taking the priest's very office away from him." Howard Kaminsky, *A History of the Hussite Revolution* (Berkeley, University of California, 1967): 124.

[6]Very suitable for parish use is *Morning and Evening* (Chicago: Liturgy Training Publications, 1996). (This work has two accompanying books. The first addresses various aspects of daily prayer in Christian history and spirituality: Joyce Ann Zimmerman, CPPS, *Morning and Evening: A Parish Celebration.* It also helps parishes begin the celebration of daily prayer. The other volume is for presiders, cantors and accompanists: *Morning and Evening: Order of Service.*)

[7]For a thorough critique and additional references, see James Dallen, *The Dilemma of Priestless Sundays* (Chicago: Liturgy Training Publications, 1994).

[8]Translation is mine.

[9]Bishops' Committee on the Permanent Diaconate, *Permanent Deacons in the United States: Guidelines on their Formation and Ministry,* (Washington: USCC, 1987): 174.

[10]"Call to Prayer: The Liturgy of the Hours," *BCL Newsletter* 13 (1977): 87–88.

[11]"A Call to Prayer," 89.

Penance: Individual or Communal?

In the past, Catholics tended to think only of individual confession as the means for forgiveness of their sins, but this singular approach to reconciliation had not always been the case in the church's history. Throughout the centuries, the baptized have sought forgiveness of their sins through a variety of ways. As Nathan Mitchell has observed:

> [T]he history of penance is the history of Christians working to discover the many opportunities for reconciliation that are revealed in the life of faith. The history of penance is a history of *diversity* and *change,* of the continuing search for a pastoral strategy that is at once realistic and compassionate, challenging and practical. This history shows clearly that Christians have found reconciliation in many different ways.[1]

The 1974 revised Rite of Penance, 4 itself recognizes a diversity of forms of penitential practices, mentioning penitential services, the proclamation of the word of God, prayer and the penitential parts of the eucharistic celebration. In his apostolic exhortation on reconciliation and penance in the mission of the church today, Pope John Paul II additionally mentions services of atonement, pilgrimages and fasting.[2]

Most Catholics in English and French-speaking North America rarely approach the sacrament of penance in its individual form anymore, perhaps doing so only once or twice a year. There are various reasons for this marked decline in individual confession of sin within the past generation. One reason is that Catholics today, as in previous centuries, find other ways to experience forgiveness. Many report that the penitential rite at the beginning of Mass satisfies their need for a rite of contrition and repentance. Clearly, there is greater recognition today of the reconciling nature of the eucharist, that worthy participation in the eucharist itself forgives venial sin and assists the Christian in leading the gospel life.

Some faithful Catholics who are weekly communicants avoid individual confession because they have had negative associations with the rite — the dark confessional box, the whispered narration of sins, perhaps a bad experience with a harsh confessor. Others have abandoned the individual rite because they find their spiritual need for repentance and absolution better met by communal celebrations of sacramental penance. Another factor, described by the pope in *Reconciliatio et Paenitentia,* 18, is the "loss of the sense of sin" that has occurred within the past generation. There doubtless has been a great change in people's perceptions about what constitutes mortal sin. This question will be explored here after first some pastoral recommendations are made on the use of the official penitential liturgies found in the Rite of Penance.

Four Penitential Rites

The Rite of Penance provides four different penitential liturgies, three sacramental rites and one form which is nonsacramental. The first is the Rite for Reconciliation of Individual Penitents, consisting of the following elements: prior preparation by both confessor and penitent; the welcoming of the penitent; a reading from the word of God; the penitent's confession and acceptance of penance; the penitent's prayer and the priest's absolution; a proclamation of praise; and dismissal of the penitent. This "Rite 1," as it is frequently called, may be shortened in parts when dictated by pastoral need. Rite 1 is also commonly referred to as "individual confession," given the fact that it is a liturgical celebration designed to be used by one confessor with only one penitent at a time.

The second rite of penance is called the Rite for Reconcilation of Several Penitents with Individual Confession and Absolution. The elements of Rite 2 are: the introductory rites, including an opening hymn, greeting and opening prayer; the celebration of the word of God with one or more readings interspersed with a psalm, a suitable song or a period of silence, followed by a homily and a period of silence for an examination of conscience; the rite of reconciliation, consisting of a common act of contrition, an optional litany or song, and the Lord's Prayer followed by individual confession, absolution and assignment of a penance. When the individual confessions are finished, the confessors return to the sanctuary and everyone makes an act of thanksgiving and praise in the form of a psalm, hymn or litany, and the service concludes with a prayer by the presider.

The third rite, the Rite for Reconcilation of Penitents with General Confession and Absolution, is structured like the second rite except that a general confession and absolution take the place of individual confession and absolution. A common penance is given to everyone, and individuals may add a further penance of their own if they wish.

Finally, the ritual provides for nonsacramental penitential services whose structure is the same as that followed in Rites 2 and 3, except that there is no confession and absolution. The presider at these services may be a deacon or a lay minister, unlike the sacramental rites, which require a priest.

The third rite, involving general confession and absolution, may only be celebrated in limited situations in accord with the policy of the diocesan bishop. There are no canonical restrictions on the use of the other rites. They should be made available with regularity so that the faithful can develop a true spirit of repentance in their lives, especially during the penitential season of Lent. The church recommends frequent recourse to the sacrament of penance because the regular examination of conscience, contrition for sin and resolve to avoid sin in the future are an aid to Christians in their vocation to holiness of life.[3]

Communal Penance

Experience in English-speaking North America within the past generation shows that the faithful generally prefer communal celebrations of penance over Rite 1, or individual confession. Attendance at communal services has remained steady, unlike the marked decline in participation in the first rite of individual confession. In some parishes the celebration of the third rite of penance attracts hundreds of people. Many of the faithful, both confessors and penitents alike, have found the third rite, when celebrated well, to be the most effective experience of sacramental penance.

Unfortunately, canon law does not permit this third official rite to be used except in quite limited situations. This restrictiveness is due to the teaching of the Council of Trent that all mortal sins ordinarily must be confessed in number and in kind in individual confession (canon 960). The third rite provides instead for a general confession and absolution, which may be validly received for venial sin, but which, in the case of serious sin, is validly received only on the condition that the penitent is suitably disposed and intends to confess individually in due time the serious sins which cannot now be confessed (canon 962, §1). This requirement confuses people who do not understand the doctrine of Trent upon which it is based.

The use of Rite 3 declined notably in the 1980s due to intense opposition to its use from certain church authorities. In some U.S. dioceses that formerly used the rite widely and routinely, forceful interventions by the bishop have succeeded in completely eliminating the use of the rite. Whether or not Rite 3 is permitted in a diocese, communal celebration of penance ought not be abandoned altogether lest important liturgical and theological values go neglected. Indeed, one could assert without exaggeration that canon law implies a preference for the communal over the individual celebration of penance.

The Second Vatican Council taught that the communal celebration of liturgical rites was normative,[4] and Pope John Paul II has taught that the *Code of Canon Law* must be interpreted in light of the Council.[5] This conciliar principle on the normativity of the communal celebration of the liturgy is found in canon law, both in the code (canon 837) and in the liturgical books, including the Rite of Penance. The latter text states in part: "Communal celebration shows more clearly the ecclesial nature of penance" (22). In various norms the rite speaks of the communal dimension, the social aspect and the ecclesial significance of penance (5, 18, 19, 22). These liturgical laws strongly imply that the communal celebration of penance better elucidates these aspects than does the individual celebration of Rite 1.

Rite 2

The second rite of sacramental penance is primarily a communal rite, but it also provides as an essential part of the rite the individual confession and absolution of sin by all present who wish to confess. In some parishes, retreat settings and other situations, the second rite has been used with great success. Those who champion this rite consider it to have the "best of both": both the communal aspect desirable for bringing out the social nature of sin and the ecclesial dimension of penance, as well as the opportunity for the liturgical action to touch each individual in a particular way.

The second rite also has its detractors, who consider it an ungainly hybrid. It is especially problematic when too many penitents participate and there are not enough confessors available to accommodate all the penitents within a reasonable time. This places the pastor or other presiding priest in a predicament. If he resorts to Rite 3 and gives a general absolution, he may risk a rebuke from his bishop. If he does not use a general absolution, many people may have to leave before receiving the sacrament and may likely be discouraged from attending future celebrations of communal penance. This dilemma has unfortunately led pastors in some places to abandon communal penance altogether, which is hardly the solution desired by the church.

On the other hand, some parishes have enjoyed great success with Rite 2. The leaders of these communities are convinced that with sufficient planning and education of the people, this form of the sacrament is the most effective and meaningful one, better even than general absolution. They acknowledge, however, that additional confessors from outside the parish are necessary to ensure that the rite proceeds expeditiously.

Other Options and Requirements

Additional priests from outside the parish for the celebration of Rite 2 are not available everywhere, particularly in rural areas. As the priest shortage worsens, one can anticipate increasing difficulty, even the impossibility in many areas, of gathering sufficient confessors for the second rite. One solution to this problem is greater use of the "fourth rite," the non-sacramental penitential service. The Rite of Penance says that penitential services are very helpful in promoting conversion of life and purification of heart. In particular, it says, these services help the faithful to prepare for individual confession that can be made later at a convenient time (37).

Instead of using Rite 2 when there are not enough confessors available, the parish staff might experiment with the penitential service, especially during the season of Lent, when these services are particularly recommended by the church,[6] but also during Advent and at other times during the year. This non-sacramental rite is a means of obtaining forgiveness for venial sin and is helpful as a preparation for Rite 1 on the part of those who need or desire it. Moreover, the presider at the fourth rite may be a deacon or lay minister, which is a distinct advantage where priests are lacking or are overworked.

Some pastors report that their people are not satisfied with a penitential service, that they expect sacramental absolution of their sins at a communal celebration and not a "mere" service of the word. Perhaps what is needed is simply to educate people to a new practice and give them time to get used to it. But this may not be a sufficient answer to the problem everywhere; it is understandable that people expect sacramental absolution and the grace of the sacrament at the time of their participation in a communal liturgy of penance.

Another solution to the problem of large crowds and insufficient confessors is to use Rite 2 but adapt it by concluding the communal part of the ceremony before individual confessions begin. Such an adaptation would be lawful in keeping with the generous provision in the rite for adaptation by priests:

> It is for priests, and especially parish priests (pastors), in celebrating reconciliation with individuals or with a community, to adapt the rite to the concrete circumstances of the penitents. They must preserve the essential structure and the entire form of absolution, but if necessary they may omit some parts of the rite for pastoral reasons or enlarge upon them.[7]

If the number of penitents is great, the concluding acts of Rite 2 (the proclamation of praise for God's mercy, the prayer of thanksgiving and the blessing, which are to be celebrated in common after individual confessions) could be omitted so that everyone would not have to stay a long time until all the penitents finish their individual confessions.

This adaptation would allow participants in the second rite the freedom to stay for individual confession, and possibly wait in long lines, or to leave without individual confession and absolution, either because they have no serious sins that they need to confess or because they will make an individual confession at a later time. The rite itself, in paragraph 22, suggests this possibility by saying: "Those who will receive the sacrament at another time may also take part in the service" [of Rite 2]. This adapted service would require that the confessors stay as long as necessary to handle all the penitents who may be waiting to confess.

The omission of the concluding parts of Rite 2 is only desirable when there are so many penitents that it would be a burden to

103

keep them waiting until all the individual confessions are heard. The ideal would be to have all penitents return to the assembly after individual confession and wait for the concluding rites to be celebrated in common, as envisioned in the ritual. However, the omission of the concluding rites is justifiable as a way of maintaining a communal celebration of the sacrament when there is no other feasible way to do it.

In some areas there are always too many penitents and too few confessors. If there is an excessive number of penitents and it would clearly be impossible to have individual confessions, even with an adaptation of Rite 2, then Rite 3 should be used in accord with the policy of the diocesan bishop, who is competent to regulate general absolution in his diocese (canon 961, §2). If a situation of serious necessity arises which has not been foreseen in the policy of the diocesan bishop, and there is no time to seek the bishop's permission in this special case, the pontifical commission that revised the code acknowledged that confessors can use general absolution in virtue of "principles of moral theology."[8] Among the principles of moral theology relevant here are excusing causes, such as physical and moral impossibility to observe the law, and *epikeia,* by which a law is not observed in a particular case in order to uphold a greater good.[9]

One adaptation not in accord with the law is the practice of announcing at a celebration of Rite 2 that the penitents are only to confess one sin or to confess only the sin that is most troubling them. While this practice is motivated by the desire to save time when there are many penitents, it violates the freedom of the penitents to confess all their sins and violates the doctrine of the Council of Trent that requires all mortal sins to be confessed.

One could satisfy the doctrinal requirement by announcing that all mortal sins must be confessed, and those who have no mortal sins should confess only those sins for which they are most sorry. However, this would not allow the penitents full freedom to tell all the venial sins they may wish to confess. It is also confusing to the many people today who do not know the difference between a mortal and a venial sin.

As with any liturgical rite, communal penance services with or without confession and absolution must be well prepared and well celebrated, with good readers, good music, good preaching and active participation. If the rite is well prepared and well celebrated, the aim of the rite will be accomplished: The faithful will be led to a sense of contrition for sin and will experience forgiveness by God through the ministry of the church, and those who have mortal sins will be motivated to seek reconcilation with God and the church through an individual and integral confession.

Individual Celebration

In many places, communal penance in one form or another is the normal way that most people now experience the sacrament of penance. Nevertheless, the first rite, a liturgical celebration involving the confessor and only one penitent at a time, should be available at least once a week in every parish, even if it is scheduled only for fifteen minutes in places where there are few penitents who desire this form.

This would seem the minimum required by canon 986, §1: "All to whom the care of souls is committed by reason of an office are obliged to provide that the confessions of the faithful entrusted to their care be heard when they reasonably ask to be heard and that the opportunity be given to them to come to individual confession on days and hours set for their convenience." The Rite of Penance, 13 similarly affirms:

> The reconciliation of penitents may be celebrated in all liturgical seasons and on any day. But it is right that the faithful be informed of the day and hours at which the priest is available for this ministry. They should be encouraged to approach the sacrament of penance at times when Mass is not being celebrated and preferably at the scheduled hours.

There should be a regular day and time each week for individual penance so that the faithful can conveniently approach the sacrament. The practice in some places, whereby confessions are only heard by appointment or only by coming to the rectory, usually results in few or no persons making use of the first rite in that parish. They either go to a neighboring parish or stop going to the individual celebration completely.

People are uneasy about making an appointment or going to the rectory for penance because either they do not want to be a bother to the priest or may desire the anonymity of the confessional, which is lost when one is forced to make an appointment or show up at the door of the priest's office. Moreover, the law requires that the sacrament ordinarily be celebrated in the confessional or reconciliation room in the church (canon 964).

Related to the place for hearing confessions is the canonical requirement that there be a fixed screen in the reconciliation room or confessional (canon 964, §2). Because many people prefer anonymity in the confessional, it is necessary that they always have the option of confessing behind a screen. Otherwise their fear of being recognized by the confessor might lead them to avoid the sacrament altogether.

Likewise, when Rite 2 is celebrated, even with a large congregation, there should always be at least one confessor behind a screen so that penitents who wish it may have the sense of anonymity that the screen provides. This is a less important concern when hearing the confessions of young children; they typically feel more comfortable speaking face-to-face with a sympathetic person than whispering behind a grille in a dark cubicle to someone they cannot see.

Mortal Sin

The law regulating sacramental penance is heavily dependent on the Council of Trent's teaching that all mortal sins must be confessed individually and integrally. However, the understanding of mortal sin in the minds of Catholic people has undergone considerable change within the past generation. Past generations of Catholics conceived of sin as objectively mortal or venial. Violations of church law — such as missing Mass on Sunday, eating meat on Friday, or a priest omitting part of the Divine Office — were considered to be objective mortal sins when they were intentionally committed without an adequate excuse. Certain other sins, such as sexual acts apart from marriage, were widely regarded as objectively grave without regard for the situation of the penitent or the nature of the circumstances.

Canonists and moral theologians today no longer equate the violation of church law with necessary sinfulness, and few moral theologians would speak of all sexual acts outside marriage as always sinful without respect to the condition of the penitent and other pertinent circumstances. Canonists recognize that sinfulness pertains to the "internal forum," the forum of conscience, whereas the observance of canon law primarily pertains to the "external forum," to the visible life of the church. It is widely taught that the faithful themselves, having examined their own informed consciences, responsibly judge the gravity of their own actions in light of the circumstances of their real life situations and the teachings of Christ and the church.

In reflecting on the gospels and the traditions of the church, especially the teachings of Thomas Aquinas, Pope John Paul II speaks of mortal sin as a rejection of God, an attitude of rebellion against or defiance of God.[10] Mortal sin is that "deadly" sin by which a person is cut off from God's grace. In committing such a sin, the person chooses death to sin rather than life with God, exercising a "fundamental option" that is against God rather than for God. The Rite of Penance, 7 speaks in similar words of "those who by grave sin have withdrawn from communion with God in love."

In truth, few practicing Catholics today perceive themselves as having committed a sin so grave that they feel cut off entirely from God's grace. Hence, they may not feel the urgency to go to individual confession, which is intended most particularly for the reconciliation of the serious sinner. The God proclaimed in today's church is more the loving and tender God of mercy than the severe and judgmental God who punishes sinners. The fear of hell for certain transgressions like missing Sunday Mass or breaking a fast is no longer a pressing concern for today's Catholic. This changed attitude most certainly has contributed to the marked decline in the frequency of individual confession.

Some theologians, as well as some bishops at the 1983 synod of bishops, suggested that an intermediate level of sinfulness ought to be recognized, namely, a sin that is serious but not mortal. Such a sin is one that troubles the penitent's conscience more seriously than the typical venial sins he or she commits but is not a sin by which the person has exercised a fundamental option against God. This idea of an intermediary level of sin corresponds to reality. Some sins, whether objectively or subjectively, are too troublesome to be merely venial but would not qualify in the penitent's mind, or perhaps even in the objective order, as a deadly sin that puts the individual outside the realm of God's grace.

Although this description of a third kind of sinfulness has merit, it is not found in canon law, which recognizes only two kinds of sin, mortal sin (also called grave or serious sin) and venial sin. Moreover, Pope John Paul II rejected this threefold classification of sins, although he did acknowledge that the triple distinction illustrates the fact that there are gradations among serious sins.[11] The pope's caution is understandable; the idea of a threefold classification of sin is still too recent for it to replace the long tradition of acknowledging only two categories of sin.

How should the difference between mortal and venial sin be understood? While truly there are gradations of serious sin, the kind of serious sin that ought to be confessed does not have to amount to a conscious decision as such to rebel against or defy God. Rather, certain acts in themselves are so serious that when deliberately chosen, they result in the loss of God's grace. On this issue John Paul II wrote:

> For mortal sin exists when a person knowingly and willingly, for whatever reason, chooses something gravely disordered. In fact, such a choice already includes contempt for the divine law, a rejection of God's love for humanity and the whole of creation: the person turns away from God and loses charity. Thus the fundamental orientation can be radically changed by individual acts.[12]

Some sins, when deliberately committed without mitigating circumstances, are objectively grave evils: for example, murder, abortion, apostasy, major theft, destruction of the environment or offensive warfare. People who have an informed conscience will have the least difficulty recognizing the difference between a mortal and a venial sin. But even those who have little formal education in religion and morals can easily learn to respect their conscience at whatever level of formation it might be.

People can be taught, even on the occasion of their examination of conscience at communal penance, that if they feel guilt for a sin and this feeling is noticeably more bothersome than the guilt they feel for their common venial sins, then they ought to treat the sin as if it were a serious matter. Objectively the sin may or may not be serious, but if the sin makes them feel serious guilt and remorse, they should regard it as if it were a serious matter. This feeling of guilt is the first step toward the recognition that the penitent needs to confess and needs to be reconciled with God and with the church.

For such sinfulness, individual confession by way of the first or second rites of sacramental penance is prescribed as normative. The experience of many centuries shows that the individual confession of sin and absolution are salutary even on the psychological level in helping consciences burdened by serious sin to experience a sense of healing, peace and reconciliation. Moreover, the church continues to teach that individual confession and absolution, even of venial sin, is a means of sacramental grace that assists the penitent in striving for a life of Christian holiness.[13]

Integral Confession

Canon 960 of the *Code of Canon Law* reflects church doctrine in stating: "Individual and integral confession and absolution constitute the only ordinary way by which the faithful person who is aware of serious sin is reconciled with God and with the church; only physical or moral impossibility excuses the person from confession of this type, in which case reconciliation can take place in other ways." Canon 988, §1 speaks more of what an integral confession of serious sin involves:

> A member of the Christian faithful is obliged to confess in kind and in number all serious sins committed after baptism and not yet directly remitted through the keys of the church nor acknowledged in individual confession, of which one is conscious after diligent examination of conscience.

An integral confession is the confession of all serious sins according to their number and kind, and the circumstances of the sin if they alter the sin's gravity. Ordinarily, serious (that is, mortal) sins are remitted only by an individual, integral confession, namely, through the first or second rites of penance. Only physical or moral impossibility excuses from this obligation to confess. For example, if no priest is available in a certain locality or if a person is impeded from getting to a confessor due to illness or old age, then it could be physically impossible to make an individual confession. An example of moral impossibility is the case of a penitent who is gravely fearful of confessing individually and cannot do so without rather serious emotional turmoil.

When either physical or moral impossibility prevents individual confession, reconciliation can occur in other ways, chiefly by general absolution or by making an act of perfect contrition. An act of perfect contrition is not the mere reciting of a set formula of contrition but rather implies a sincere feeling of contrition and the resolve to amend one's life and make reparation for any harm that may have been done to another by the sin.

A person in serious sin is prohibited from receiving holy communion, but canon 916, after spelling out this rule, gives an exception to it. Whenever the faithful who are in serious sin are present for the celebration of the eucharist, and they have a grave reason for desiring to receive holy communion, they may do so provided they make an act of perfect contrition, including the intention of confessing the serious sin or sins as soon as possible. Some examples of grave reasons for receiving communion may be the nature of the occasion, such as a special family celebration or a great feast, or grave embarrassment and shame that would be suffered if the person did not receive communion together with the others present. As in the case of receiving general absolution (canon 962, §1), the penitent must intend to confess the serious sin or sins as soon as possible. This upholds the teaching of the Council of Trent requiring that all serious sins be confessed in number and in kind.

Conclusion

The church recognizes a variety of ways that the faithful can obtain forgiveness of their sins. Canon law, including the laws in the liturgical books, acknowledges this variety. Among these ways to forgiveness, the Rite of Penance provides four distinct forms of liturgical celebrations, three sacramental and one non-sacramental.

Those in charge of pastoral care in parishes and other communities should offer the faithful regular opportunities for the celebration of both the individual and communal rites of penance. Individual confession is necessary for the absolution of mortal sins unless physical or moral impossibility excuses from this type of penance. The individual rite is also a helpful penitential discipline for growth in holiness of life, even for those who have no mortal sins to confess.

Communal penance ought to be the normative liturgical experience of penance, since all liturgical celebrations, by their very nature, are ecclesial actions. The rite or rites of communal penance celebrated with the community should be in keeping with the number of penitents and confessors who usually attend; other circumstances and needs should also be considered in the choice of rite and its possible adaptation. Liturgical law permits the ministers to make adaptations in the rites to accommodate local situations. With the variety of forms of communal penance and the generous provision for adaptation allowed by liturgical law, one or more forms of communal penance can be regularly offered in every parish or other community, even in areas without sufficient confessors.

NOTES

[1]*The Rite of Penance: Commentaries, Background and Directions,* ed. Nathan Mitchell (Washington: The Liturgical Conference, 1978): 36. See also p. 78. For other useful studies on penance, see Ladislas Örsy, *The Evolving Church and the Sacrament of Penance* (Denville, NJ: Dimension Books, 1978); Paul J. Roy, Denis J. Woods, Peter E. Fink and Walter H. Cuenin, *Alternative Futures for Worship* 4: *Reconciliation,* series ed. Peter E. Fink (Collegeville: The Liturgical Press, 1987); *Reconciliation: The Continuing Agenda,* ed. Robert J. Kennedy (Collegeville: The Liturgical Press, 1987); Lawrence E. Mick, *Penance: The Once and Future Sacrament* (Collegeville: The Liturgical Press, 1987); *Confession and Absolution,* ed. Martin Dudley and Geoffrey Rowell (Collegeville: The Liturgical Press, 1990).

[2]*Reconciliatio et paenitentia,* 28; December 2, 1984, AAS 77 (1985): 185–275; *Origins* 14 (1984): 432–58.

[3]*Reconciliatio et Paenitentia,* 32; canons 987, 988.

[4]SC, 14, 26, 27, 48.

[5]Apostolic constitution *Sacrae disciplinae leges,* January 25, 1983, AAS 75 (1983): vi–xiv. Translations of the apostolic constitution appear at the beginning of all vernacular translations of the *Code of Canon Law.*

[6]Circular letter on preparing and celebrating the paschal feasts *Paschalis sollemnitatis,* 13, 37, January 26, 1988, *Notitiae* 24 (1988): 81–107; *Origins* 17 (1988): 677–87; Ceremonial of Bishops, 251.

[7]Paragraph 40a; translations of the Rite of Penance are by ICEL.

[8]Pontifical Commission for the Revision of the Code of Canon Law, response, *Communicationes* 15 (1983): 206.

[9]Lawrence J. Riley, *The History, Nature and Use of Epikeia in Moral Theology* (Washington, D.C.: Catholic University of America, 1948); Frederick R. McManus, "Liturgical Law and Difficult Cases," *Worship* 48 (1974): 347–66; John Huels, *The Pastoral Companion: A Canon Law Handbook for Catholic Ministry,* 2nd ed. rev. (Quincy, IL: Franciscan Press, 1995): 12–14.

[10]*Reconciliatio et Paenitentiae,* 17.

[11]Ibid.

[12]Ibid.

[13]Canon 988, §2; *Reconciliatio et Paenitentiae,* 32.

Sacramental Sharing with Other Christians

A new spirit of good will and rapprochement between Catholics and other Christians, ushered in by the Second Vatican Council, has borne fruit in many areas, including theological dialogue, shared worship and cooperation in ministry and social programs. In the late 1980s and early 1990s, it had appeared to many that ecumenical progress was at a standstill, at least as far as official Roman Catholic contributions were concerned. However, this pessimism eased considerably with the publication of the 1993 *Directory for the Application of Principles and Norms on Ecumenism*[1] and Pope John Paul II's encyclical on ecumenism and apostolic letter on the Eastern churches, both published in 1995.[2] The twentieth century is already being dubbed by some church persons as the "ecumenical century." The remarkable ecumenical progress made during the twentieth century, especially since Vatican II, has intensified desires for a hastening of that day when Christ's ecclesial body will be restored to the unity he intended it to have. This has been an especially strong desire of Pope John Paul II, and it recurs repeatedly in his encyclical on ecumenism, *Ut unum sint!* — "that they may be one!"

Many Christians of various denominations are convinced that a policy of open communion, or intercommunion,[3] can be an effective means toward the goal of restoring visible unity to Christ's body, the church. They believe that the willingness to resolve differences is strengthened when Christians gather together around the Lord's table to partake of the one bread and one cup. However, the official policy of the Catholic Church opposes intercommunion as a means toward Christian unity; it does not, though, exclude all forms of sacramental sharing. The Catholic position is that sharing in the eucharist is a sign of a real unity achieved and is not to be a means toward that unity.

From Vatican II to the Code

Vatican II offered the opportunity for sharing in worship and sacraments *(communicatio in sacris)* with other Christian denominations under certain conditions. Derogating from the 1917 *Code of Canon Law* (canon 731, §2), which had outlawed the administration of sacraments to non-Catholics, the *Decree on Ecumenism* established the general principle that although *communicatio in sacris* "may not be regarded as a means to be used indiscriminately toward restoring Christian unity . . . its being a source of grace sometimes favors it."[4] The council was particularly open to sacramental sharing with Eastern Christians: "Because these churches, even though separated from us, have true sacraments and especially, by virtue of apostolic succession, the eucharist and the priesthood — all bonds still linking them closely to us — some form of *communicatio in sacris* is not only admissible but even advisable in the right circumstances and with the approval of church authority" (UR, 15; DOL, 187). The policy for sacramental sharing with the Eastern Christians was specified by the council in its *Decree on the Oriental Churches:*

[W]hen Eastern Christians separated in good faith from the Catholic Church request it of their own accord and are rightly disposed, they may be admitted to the sacraments of penance, eucharist and anointing of the sick. Moreover, Catholics may request these same sacraments of ministers of other Eastern churches having valid sacraments on any occasion of need or genuine spiritual benefit when access to a Catholic priest is physically or morally impossible.[5]

The policy for sacramental sharing with Protestants, enunciated by the Secretariat for Promoting Christian Unity in the 1967 *Ecumenical Directory,* is much more restrictive. It prohibits Protestants from receiving the eucharist, as well as penance and anointing of the sick, except on an individual basis in situations of pressing need such as danger of death and persecution and in prisons, and only when such persons do not have access to a minister of their own communion and ask on their own to receive the sacraments. Furthermore, there must be a sign of both their belief in these sacraments consonant with the faith of the church and also their proper disposition. As for Catholics receiving communion from Protestant ministers, the 1967 Directory stated that Catholics in similar circumstances may request these sacraments only of a minister who is validly ordained.[6]

Although great advances in ecumenism occurred during the almost two decades between the promulgation of the *Decree on Ecumenism* and the revised *Code of Canon Law,* the church's revised law book by and large simply codified the existing discipline on *communicatio in sacris* without any significant changes. In the revised *Ecumenical Directory* of 1993, however, there was an important development: For the first time, the Holy See stated that a Protestant party, in accord with canon law, might receive holy communion at his or her wedding Mass and even occasionally during the course of the marriage. We will look at these developments in this chapter, but first we will review the general discipline of the Catholic Church on sacramental sharing as it is established in the *Code of Canon Law.* This is necessary because the *Ecumenical Directory* must be interpreted in a way that is consistent with the law. We will also make reference to the 1990 *Code of Canons of the Eastern Churches,* which gives the law common to all the Catholic Eastern churches.

The discipline on sacramental sharing is found in canon 844 in the Latin code and canon 671 in the Eastern code. Because the two canons are nearly identical, we will only refer to canon 844 with the understanding that it is also applicable to canon 671. Canon 844 is a lengthy and complicated canon consisting of five paragraphs. The first paragraph establishes the general principle that Catholic ministers may licitly administer the sacraments only to Catholics and that Catholics may licitly receive the sacraments only from Catholic ministers. Paragraph 5 states another general principle, the principle that diocesan bishops and episcopal conferences are not to enact general norms on sacramental sharing except after consulting the competent authority, at least the local authority, of the interested non-Catholic church or community. The other three paragraphs treat (1) the reception by Catholics of the sacrament of penance, eucharist and anointing of the sick from a non-Catholic minister, (2) the administration of these same three sacraments by a Catholic minister to Eastern Christians and their canonical equivalents, and (3) the administration of the same three sacraments to Protestants. We will discuss these three latter paragraphs by first considering paragraphs 3 and 4 on the administration of the eucharist, penance, and anointing of the sick to non-Catholics and then returning to paragraph 2, on the reception of these sacraments by Catholics from a non-Catholic minister.

Administration of Sacraments to Eastern Christians

Canon 844, §3. Catholic ministers may licitly administer the sacraments of penance, eucharist and anointing of the sick to members of the Oriental churches which do not have full communion with the Catholic Church, if they ask on their own for the sacraments and are properly disposed. This holds also for members of other churches, which in the judgment of the Apostolic See are in the same condition as the Oriental churches as far as these sacraments are concerned.

This law refers to the administration of the sacraments of penance, eucharist and anointing of the sick to members of Eastern non-Catholic churches and churches with an equivalent ecclesial status. Although the *Decree on Ecumenism,* 13 singled out the Anglican communion as having "a special place among those communions in which Catholic traditions and institutions in part continue to exist," the Apostolic See has not made a formal judgment concerning the Anglican communion or other communions as a church or churches in the same condition as the Oriental churches. However, the conditions for being such a church were clarified by the Vatican Secretariat for Promoting Christian Unity. Such are the churches that "have preserved the substance of the eucharistic teaching, the sacrament of orders, and apostolic succession."[7] An example is the Polish National Church.

The law of canon 844, §3 requires that two conditions be fulfilled before members of such churches may receive the eucharist from a Catholic minister: They must ask on their own for the sacrament, and they must be properly disposed. The first condition is clear enough; the request for the sacrament must be spontaneous, that is, not at the instigation of the Catholic minister. This requirement of the law is pastorally wise and ecumenically sensitive. If, for example, at the eucharist on some special occasion, the Catholic priest would publicly invite some Orthodox persons who are present to receive communion, it would put them in a very embarrassing position if they did not wish to receive. Some Orthodox churches do not approve of intercommunion with Catholics,[8] and they generally are not accustomed to communicating as frequently as Catholics. Thus, the better solution is for the Catholic minister — at an appropriate time apart from the eucharist — to explain the openness of the Catholic Church to sacramental sharing with the Orthodox. In the case of an Orthodox-Catholic wedding, for example, the minister could inform the Catholic party of the church's practice and let the Catholic party speak to the Orthodox. Then the Orthodox party will have greater liberty to ask for the sacrament spontaneously and will not be put in the awkward position of having to decline the Catholic minister's invitation should that party not wish to receive.

The second condition for an Eastern Christian or member of an equivalent church to receive penance, eucharist or anointing of the sick is to have the proper disposition. The proper disposition is necessary for the reception of any sacrament. One must be in the state of grace and have the intention of receiving the sacrament. But who is to make the judgment that this disposition is lacking? Because one's disposition is a matter of the internal forum, generally known only to persons themselves, usually the minister of the eucharist has no way of knowing whether a person has the proper disposition or not. Therefore, the minister must presume that a person who approaches the sacrament has the proper disposition unless there is contrary evidence based on public knowledge.

Because mixed marriages are very common in North America, they can serve as a useful example in considering the meaning of the requirement of proper disposition in the case of an Eastern Christian's decision to receive communion at a wedding Mass. In the course of preparation for marriage, the priest, deacon or lay minister frequently gets to know the couple fairly well and learns of the faith level of each party, whether they are in good standing in their own church, how regularly they practice and what a church wedding means to them. Such knowledge can be helpful in determining whether a wedding Mass should be recommended or it would be preferable to follow the Rite of Marriage Outside Mass. If both parties practice their faith, a wedding Mass with communion would be desirable. If, however, the Eastern party is not a practicing Christian, it would often be better to follow the Rite of Marriage Outside Mass rather than have to deny communion to the Eastern Christian, who may lack the proper disposition, while giving it to the Catholic party, who is properly disposed.

Administration of Sacraments to Protestants

While the church's law is open to allowing Eastern Christians and members of canonically equivalent churches to receive penance, eucharist and anointing of the sick from a Catholic minister, it is quite restrictive in the case of those baptized Christians who belong to other ecclesial communities, namely, Protestants. Canon 844, §4 states:

> If the danger of death is present or other grave necessity, in the judgment of the diocesan bishop or the conference of bishops, Catholic ministers may licitly administer these sacraments to other Christians who do not have full communion with the Catholic Church, who cannot approach a

> minister of their own community and on their own ask for it, provided they
> manifest Catholic faith in these sacraments and are properly disposed.

Instead of the diocesan bishop and the episcopal conference, canon 671, §4 of the Eastern code speaks of their Eastern equivalents, the eparchial bishop and the synod of bishops of the patriarchal church or the council of hierarchs.

The conditions of this law on the administration of the three sacraments in question to Protestants are far more restrictive than the preceding paragraph governing the Eastern Christians. Not only must Protestants ask for the sacrament on their own and be properly disposed, but they also must be in danger of death or there must be some other grave necessity which is judged to be such by the diocesan bishop or by the episcopal conference. Further, they must be unable to approach a minister of their own community and must manifest a Catholic faith in these sacraments.

Canon 844, §3 implicitly allows the minister of the sacrament to determine whether an Eastern Christian meets all the conditions to receive it, but in the case of Protestants, it is not the minister but higher episcopal authority who has this competence. Ordinarily the three sacraments may be administered to Protestants only in cases permitted by the diocesan bishop or by the episcopal conference unless it is a question of danger of death. On this point, the 1993 *Ecumenical Directory,* 130 states that in cases other than the danger of death

> [I]t is strongly recommended that the diocesan bishop, taking into account
> any norms which may have been established for this matter by the epis-
> copal conference or by the synods of Eastern Catholic churches, establish
> general norms for judging situations of grave and pressing need. . . .
> Catholic ministers will judge individual cases and administer these sacra-
> ments only in accord with these established norms, where they exist.
> Otherwise they will judge according to the norms of this Directory.

In the absence of a general policy established by the episcopal conference, each diocesan bishop can determine what cases constitute spiritual or material necessity. Moreover, even when cases have been determined by the episcopal conference, the diocesan bishop is free to add other general cases or grant special permission for cases not envisioned.

In some dioceses there is no policy on sacramental sharing. But the Holy See itself has enunciated several cases of grave need besides danger of death. In a 1972 instruction, the Secretariat for Promoting Christian Unity determined that cases of grave need for administering sacraments to Protestants include situations of persecution, persons imprisoned and when non-Catholic Christians live in an area where they do not have access to a minister of their own ecclesial community.[9] The instruction affirmed that cases of grave necessity include spiritual as well as material need. It stated further that the *Ecumenical Directory* grants to episcopal authority "quite broad powers of decision" in judging whether the necessary conditions are present for these cases. This also applies to the revised *Ecumenical Directory* of 1993.

The 1993 Directory itself mentions two new cases when non-Catholic Christians, not excluding Protestants, might receive permission to receive the Catholic eucharist. One is at their wedding Mass in a mixed marriage to a Catholic. The revised Directory, 159 states: "[T]he decision as to whether the non-Catholic party of the marriage may be admitted to eucharistic communion is to be made in keeping with the general norms existing in the matter both for Eastern Christians and for other Christians, taking into account the particular situation of the reception of the sacrament of Christian marriage by two baptized Christians." This is the first time that a public document from the Holy See has acknowledged that a mixed marriage can be a case of "grave necessity," as required by canon 844, §4, whereby the diocesan bishop or the episcopal conference can permit the Protestant party to receive holy communion. This is, indeed, a considerable broadening of the notion of "grave necessity," one that understands such necessity to include cases of spiritual need on an important occasion. The Protestant party, of course, would have to meet the other requirements of the law, namely, asking for the sacrament on his or her own, manifesting a Catholic faith in it and being properly disposed.

There is a problem with celebrating a mixed marriage between a Catholic and a Protestant at the eucharist that is not resolved in the revised *Ecumenical Directory*. Although the

Protestant party to the marriage might be eligible to receive communion at the wedding Mass, the other Protestant guests are not. Consequently, the eucharist at a marriage between a Catholic and a Protestant "marks a division in a congregation assembled to celebrate a sacramental union."[10] Even if the non-Catholic spouse is given permission to receive communion, it would not be possible to allow the Protestant family and other Protestant guests to receive, since there would be no way to determine whether they fulfill all the conditions required by canon 844, §4. Ordinarily, therefore, it is pastorally and ecumenically preferable not to celebrate the eucharist at a wedding between a Catholic and a Protestant.[11]

The 1993 *Ecumenical Directory,* 160 manifests an openness to eucharistic sharing also on an occasional basis by a baptized non-Catholic in a mixed marriage during the course of the marriage, in accord with the provisions of canon 844. "Although the spouses in a mixed marriage share the sacraments of baptism and marriage, eucharistic sharing can only be exceptional." When both parties share substantially the Catholic faith in the eucharist and are practicing Christians, their sharing in the eucharist at the Lord's table on special occasions during the course of their marriage can be a rich symbol of the union of their lives and of communion with the whole church. Because the nature and frequency of these special cases may vary greatly from couple to couple, it would be better if a diocesan policy simply stated the case in broad terms and allowed the couple to determine the specific cases of spiritual need as they saw fit.

Another requirement for administering the sacraments of penance, eucharist or anointing of the sick to Protestants is that they not have access to their own minister. Does this mean that the Protestant never has access to his or her own minister or that he or she does not at this moment have access, or does it mean something in between? A long-standing canonical axiom holds that "favors are to be multiplied, burdens are to be restricted." Favorable laws may be interpreted broadly, but laws which restrict rights must be strictly interpreted. Because this canon has the nature of a favor in permitting the three sacraments in question to be administered to Protestants, it calls for broad interpretation. For example, an elderly Protestant resident is attending a Catholic

Mass in a nursing home chapel. She does not have access to her own minister without leaving the nursing home; this is difficult or seriously inconvenient. In such a situation, broad interpretation of the law would conclude that access to the Protestant minister is morally impossible, even though the minister resides in the locality.

Another condition of the law for administering any of the three sacraments to Protestants is that they must manifest the Catholic faith in the sacrament. A communication of the Secretariat for Promoting Christian Unity stated: "For admission of other Christians to the eucharist in the Catholic Church . . . they must give signs of a faith consistent with the Catholic Church's faith regarding this sacrament. Such faith does not consist simply in the acceptance of the real presence but implies as well the doctrine on the eucharist as taught by the Catholic church."[12] In dealing with this condition, it is necessary to keep in mind that the law does not require a detailed knowledge of Catholic eucharistic doctrine. Such knowledge is not required of Catholic communicants, so it follows that the church does not expect more from non-Catholics than it does from its own members. Rather, the law requires that the non-Catholic manifest a Catholic *faith*. Can the person assent to the substance of Catholic doctrine? To determine this, it would usually suffice for the minister to receive an affirmative answer to questions like: Do you believe that what the Catholic church teaches about the eucharist is true? In particular, do you believe that the consecrated bread and wine is the body and blood of the Lord? The person need not know about specific theories or doctrines such as transubstantiation. Moreover, it often would not even be necessary to question persons belonging to some of the mainline Protestant churches, such as the Anglican (Episcopal) and Lutheran, whose contemporary theology of the eucharist is very similar to that of the Catholics.[13]

Reception of Sacraments from Non-Catholic Ministers

Canon 844 §2. Whenever necessity requires or genuine spiritual advantage suggests, and provided that the danger of error or indifferentism is avoided, it is lawful for the faithful for whom it is physically or morally impossible to approach a Catholic minister to receive the sacraments of penance, eucharist and anointing of the sick from non-Catholic ministers in whose churches these sacraments are valid.

Like paragraphs 3 and 4 of canon 844, discussed in the previous section, this norm is an exception to the basic rule of paragraph 1 of the canon that Catholics can receive sacraments only from Catholic ministers. Here the law permits Catholics to receive the three sacraments in question from a non-Catholic minister under certain conditions. An initial condition is that the case be one of necessity or genuine spiritual advantage. The Catholics who wish to receive can themselves determine whether this condition is fulfilled. If a Catholic, for example, is attending the divine liturgy at an Orthodox church and believes that it would be spiritually advantageous to receive, then this requirement has been met. However, Catholics should be sensitive to the views and practices of the other church. The discipline of Eastern Christian churches often is not as open to sacramental sharing with Catholics as is Catholic law with them. The 1993 *Ecumenical Directory,* 24 expresses this sensitivity:

> Since practice differs between Catholics and Eastern Christians in the matter of frequent communion, confession before communion and the eucharistic fast, care must be taken to avoid scandal and suspicion among Eastern Christians through Catholics not following the Eastern usage. A Catholic who legitimately wishes to communicate with Eastern Christians must respect the Eastern discipline as much as possible and refrain from communicating if that church restricts sacramental communion to its own members to the exclusion of others.

A second condition for a Catholic to receive sacraments in a non-Catholic church is that the danger of error or indifferentism must be avoided. Such would be the erroneous view on the part of the Catholic that there is no real difference between the churches and that it does not matter where one worships, even to the neglect of the practice of one's faith.

A third condition is the physical or moral impossibility of approaching a Catholic minister. In this context, moral impossibility does not mean that the Catholic is physically prevented from approaching a Catholic minister but that it would be impossible to do so without serious inconvenience or personal disadvantage. Some examples would include the case of a Catholic in a country where the church is persecuted; or a Catholic living in an area where there is only one Catholic church and that person is unable to go there for one reason or another, such as in the case of a divorced and remarried person who wishes to receive communion but wants to avoid scandal. Cases of physical impossibility are potentially many: the absence of a Catholic minister in the area, situations of imprisonment, persecution, hospitalization, etc. The meaning of physical or moral impossibility is subject to broad interpretation. For example, a Catholic who attends a eucharistic liturgy on a special occasion in a non-Catholic church truly has a physical impossibility of receiving communion from a Catholic minister at that eucharist; therefore, if the other conditions of the law are met, it would be licit to receive on that occasion.

The last condition mentioned is the most restrictive of them all, because it rules out any reception of the three sacraments from ecclesial communities in which these sacraments are not valid. Canon law requires for validity that the sacraments of penance, eucharist and anointing of the sick be celebrated by a validly ordained priest. Only those who are ordained by a bishop in apostolic succession are considered by the Catholic church to be validly ordained. According to traditional practice, this would exclude reception of communion in all Protestant churches, unless a Protestant priest has valid orders according to Catholic standards; this may very well be the case with the Anglican clergy. For the most part, then, the law permits Catholics to receive the eucharist only from the Eastern churches and their legal equivalents, as has been discussed.

Conclusion

Since Vatican II there have been small but significant changes in the church's laws regulating the administration of the sacraments of penance, eucharist and anointing of the sick to non-Catholics and their reception by Catholics from non-Catholic ministers. The 1983 *Code of Canon Law* codified the prevailing discipline found in conciliar and post-conciliar documents. The 1993 *Ecumenical Directory* added two new cases for sacramental sharing in addition to those proposed in a 1972 instruction of the Secretariat for Promoting Christian Unity. Canon 844 of the Latin code and canon 671 of the Eastern code display a relative openness to sharing in the sacraments of penance, eucharist and anointing of the sick with Eastern non-Catholic churches and their canonical equivalents, such as the Polish National Church, Old Catholics and Old Roman Catholics. Protestants, on the other hand, may receive the three sacraments in the Catholic Church only in cases of grave need as determined by the episcopal conference, the Eastern Catholic synod of bishops, the diocesan bishop, or, in the absence of particular norms, in light of the cases and principles established by the Holy See.

Catholics are more severely limited in their possibilities for receiving sacraments from non-Catholic ministers. Most restrictive of all is the condition that Catholics may only receive in those churches which have a valid eucharist; thus Catholics are limited for the most part to receiving communion in the Eastern churches, which frequently do not permit sacramental sharing anyway.

Behind the restrictions in the law is the Catholic teaching that sacramental sharing, particularly sharing in the eucharist, is not to be taken as a means toward Christian unity but is to be considered a sign of an actual unity already achieved. The Catholic position is that sharing in the eucharist on a regular basis can only come about when solutions to doctrinal differences can be reached and the Catholic church can recognize the other church as sharing its own faith.

Although sacramental sharing is restricted by canon law, the church strongly promotes ecumenical prayer, dialogue and many kinds of cooperation with other Christians as important means toward the goal of Christian unity. The 1993 *Ecumenical Directory* provides a blueprint for participation by all Catholics in the ecumenical movement. Pope John Paul II himself has provided the example. On nearly every pastoral trip, he has at least once gathered for prayer with other Christian leaders in the area. In his 1995 encyclical *Ut unum sint!* the pope repeatedly urged that every Christian should work for Christian unity by means of prayer, repentance and conversion. He recognizes that

> due to disagreements in matters of faith, it is not yet possible to celebrate together the same eucharistic liturgy. And yet we do have a burning desire to join in celebrating the one eucharist of the Lord, and this desire itself is already a common prayer of praise, a single supplication. . . . The power of God's Spirit gives growth and builds up the church down the centuries. As the church turns her gaze toward the new millennium, she asks the Spirit for the grace to strengthen her own unity and to make it grow toward full communion with other Christians. (45, 102)

The pope's hopeful prayer encourages optimism that, despite ecumenical setbacks and theological intransigence, at some future point now unknown the visible unity of Christ's church will be restored and all Christians will share as one body in the one bread and the one cup at the table of the Lord.

NOTES

[1]Directoire pour l'application des principes et des normes sur l'oecumenisme, March 25, 1993, AAS 85 (1993): 1039–1119; *Origins* 23 (1993): 129–60.

[2]*Ut unum sint!,* May 25, 1995, *Origins* 25 (1995): 49–72; *Orientale lumen,* May 2, 1995, AAS 87 (1995): 745–74; *Origins* 25 (1995): 1–13.

[3]"Open communion" is a more felicitous term than "intercommunion," since the latter implies reciprocation. However, "intercommunion" will be used here, since it is better known, with the understanding that reciprocation is not implied.

[4]*Unitatis redintegratio,* 8, November 21, 1964, AAS 57 (1965): 90–107; DOL, 186.

[5]*Orientalium Ecclesiarum,* 27, November 21, 1964, AAS 57 (1965): 76–85; DOL, 179.

[6]*Ad totam Ecclesiam,* 55, May 14, 1967, AAS 59 (1967): 574–92; DOL, 1009.

[7]Communication *Dopo la pubblicazione,* 9, October 17, 1973, AAS 65 (1973): 616–19; DOL, 1061.

[8]J. Madey, "Intercommunion Between Catholics and Orthodox," *Diakonia* 7 (1972): 73–76.

[9]*In quibus rerum circumstantiis,* 6, June 1, 1972, AAS 64 (1972): 518–25; DOL, 1050.

[10]Aelred Tegels, "Chronicle," *Worship* 59 (1985): 446.

[11]For further treatment of this issue, the reader is referred to the essay, "Mixed Marriages in the Eucharist," in my previous volume, *Disputed Questions in the Liturgy Today* (Chicago: Liturgy Training Publications, 1988).

[12]*Dopo la pubblicazzione,* 7, October 17, 1973; DOL, 1059.

[13]See Anglican-Roman Catholic International Commission, *The Final Report* (Washington: USCC, 1982); *Lutherans and Catholics in Dialogue,* vol. 4: *Eucharist and Ministry* (Washington: USCC, 1970). See also Faith and Order Commission of the World Council of Churches, Paper no. 111, *Baptism, Eucharist, and Ministry,* 1982.

Reception of Sacraments by Divorced and Remarried Persons

The Catholic Church teaches that, ordinarily, persons in irregular unions may not be admitted to the sacraments, chiefly the sacraments of penance and eucharist. Their marital unions are considered irregular because they could not be validly married as a result of the fact that one of them, or both of them, had been previously married and the previous spouse or spouses are still living. The previous marriage brings about the divine law impediment of *ligamen,* or prior bond (canon 1085; CCEC, 802), which is founded upon Christ's command in the gospel that what God has joined together in marriage cannot be divided.[1] The impediment of prior bond prohibits marriage as long as the previous spouse is still living, and so a subsequent marriage is invalid. Since this is a divine law, it binds everyone, Catholics and non-Catholics alike. For example, when two non-Catholics divorce and remarry, the Catholic church considers their second marriages invalid, just as if a Catholic were to be married again while the previous spouse was still living.

Following the 1980 synod of bishops, which treated the family, Pope John Paul II affirmed the church's practice of not admitting to eucharistic communion persons in irregular marriages. In his apostolic exhortation on the family, *Familiaris consortio,* he wrote: "They are unable to be admittted thereto from the fact that their state and condition of life objectively contradict that union of love between Christ and the church which is signified and effected by the eucharist." He added a second reason of a pastoral nature for the traditional prohibition: "If these people were admitted to the eucharist, the faithful would be led into error and confusion regarding the church's teaching about the indissolubility of marriage."[2] The pope repeated this teaching following the 1983 synod on reconciliation in his apostolic exhortation on reconciliation and penance, *Reconciliatio et Paenitentia.* He said that those in irregular unions may "approach the divine mercy by other ways, not however through the sacraments of penance and the eucharist until such time as they have attained the required dispositions."[3]

Although these statements appear to admit of no exceptions, the church has long permitted divorced and remarried Catholics to return to the sacraments — even without an annulment or dissolution of the previous marriage — by means of the so-called "internal forum solution." The internal forum refers to matters of conscience, the private realm of a person's thoughts, actions and sins that are not publicly known. It pertains to private and secret matters, for example, whatever is said in a sacramental confession or in spiritual direction. These are matters that are completely confidential and cannot be revealed by a priest or other minister. In contrast, the external forum pertains to matters which are publicly known or can be publicly known. Most of church life and canon law operates in the external forum. For example, the fact that a marriage is invalid for reason of prior bond is a matter of the external forum, capable of proof by documentary evidence and witness testimony. In the "internal forum solution," an invalid marriage remains invalid in the external forum and cannot be made valid without an annulment as long as a prior spouse is still living; but if the person's conscience is clear, he or she may receive the sacraments despite being in an invalid marriage. In the public arena, in the external forum, the person is living in an objective state of sinfulness; but in the internal forum, in the "eyes of God," the person is convinced in conscience of being properly disposed for the reception of holy communion.

In 1994 the Congregation for the Doctrine of the Faith issued a letter to bishops in which it expressed objections to certain new pastoral approaches to the reconciliation of divorced and remarried Catholics. This has caused some confusion about whether the internal forum solution may still be used. But in fact, both Pope John Paul II and the CDF recognize the legitimacy of the internal forum solution. The issue disputed is the extent of its applicability. In the traditional understanding, the couple in an irregular marriage who wish to return to the sacraments must live as "brother and sister," that is, without sexual relations. The reason for this is that since one or both of them are still held by the bond of a previous marriage, they would be committing the sin of adultery by having sexual intercourse with their present partner, who is not their valid spouse. However, some newer approaches to the internal forum solution do not demand that a couple abandon sexual relations.

During the period from the late 1960s through the 1980s, the internal forum solution was widely discussed and debated in academic and pastoral circles.[4] Many Catholics had hoped that the 1980 synod would lead to some change in the church's practice that would officially broaden the possibilities for sacramental reception for the divorced and remarried. In 1993 three German bishops issued a joint pastoral letter providing common guidelines for the pastoral care of persons who are divorced and remarried, including criteria for the use of the internal forum solution. The question will doubtless continue to foster debate among Catholic authorities, academics and pastoral ministers.

In this essay we will summarize the position of the three German bishops in their 1993 pastoral letter, the position of the 1994 letter of the CDF, and the response of the three German bishops to the CDF. The pastoral letter of the German bishops provides a good example of the new approach to the application

of the internal forum solution that has been discussed by
scholars and in some places quietly implemented in pastoral
practice. The CDF letter, in contrast, makes the case for the traditional approach. Following the summary of the three documents,
we will continue the discussion with some further reflections
on the issue.

Solutions in the External Forum

Before considering the questions involved with the use of the
internal forum solution, it must be stated that a resolution to the
problem of sacramental reception by the divorced and remarried
in the *external forum* is preferable and should always be
attempted if possible before resorting to the internal forum. This
means that the person who was previously married should try
to obtain an annulment of the previous marriage from a Catholic
marriage tribunal. Another option in the external forum exists
when the previous marriage was a non-sacramental marriage,
meaning that one or both parties were not baptized. In such
a case a dissolution of the previous marriage may be possible
even without its being declared invalid. In rare cases when
the marriage is not consummated, even a sacramental marriage
may be dissolved.

In most areas of North America, diocesan tribunals are well
staffed and function efficiently. Developments in jurisprudence
and law have created greater opportunities for annulment than
were possible in past generations. Many divorced and remarried
persons remain unaware of this progress and are often convinced
that they have no grounds for a case. Sometimes such persons
were even told by a priest not expert in canon law that they did
not have a case. Not all priests, deacons and other pastoral
ministers can be expected to have detailed knowledge about developments in the church's marriage law and jurisprudence. Consequently, the best advice for such ministers is never to
discourage anyone from presenting a petition to the tribunal.
When priests or other ministers responsible for pastoral care are
not capable themselves of assisting divorced and remarried
persons to prepare a petition, they should at least counsel such

persons to talk with a tribunal official or canonist to determine whether there may be grounds for a case.

Many persons who could benefit from a solution in the external forum also fail to take advantage of this avenue due to unfounded fears of the tribunal process and mistaken notions about it. They believe that the case will take years to adjudicate, that it will be very expensive for them, that only the influential can get annulments, that they risk losing confidentiality, that their children will be rendered illegitimate, and so forth. Despite efforts to dispel such myths,[5] they still seem to persist rather widely. The need is great to reach out to the divorced and remarried and to encourage them to seek some resolution of their situation in the external forum by means of an annulment or dissolution of their and/or their spouse's previous marriage. This task is time-consuming and burdensome to busy parish priests, but unless more deacons and laity are trained in canon law, it will largely be their responsibility to see that this important service is offered.

An external forum solution by means of an annulment or dissolution will be possible in the majority of cases. However, sometimes a tribunal will not accept a party's case due to lack of evidence in favor of nullity. Sometimes, also, the tribunal or appeals court will render a negative judgment and deny the annulment. Moreover, it may happen that one party to the irregular marriage cannot prevail upon the other spouse, who had previously been married, to seek an annulment. This is more likely to occur when a Catholic marries a divorced non-Catholic who may be hostile to or suspicious of the Catholic church's annulment process. If for any reason an annulment or dissolution of a previous marriage is not possible or feasible, the confessor, spiritual adviser or parish minister should consider the option of exploring with the Catholic party or parties to the irregular marriage the option known as the internal forum solution. Unlike an external forum solution, the internal forum solution cannot lead to the convalidation of the invalid union; its sole purpose is to enable Catholics in an irregular union to return to the sacraments, especially the eucharist.

A Pastoral Approach in Germany

In 1993 a pastoral letter on ministering to divorced and remarried couples was issued by the three bishops of the ecclesiastical province of the Upper Rhine in Germany: Bishop Karl Lehmann of Mainz, president of the German bishops' conference, Archbishop Oskar Saier of Freiburg, conference vice president, and Bishop Walter Kasper of Ruttenburg-Stuttgart (who is an internationally known theologian).[6] In preparing their pastoral letter, the three bishops drew upon a wealth of scholarship and pastoral initiatives undertaken in the past several decades. The bishops began their letter by addressing the situation of divorced and remarried Christians today. Divorced people, the bishops wrote, often feel that the church and society lack an understanding of their problems; they feel discriminated against, cast out, even condemned; they find the church's rules incomprehensibly hard and merciless.

Next, the bishops address the teaching on marriage established by Jesus in the gospel. They put his words in the context of his teaching on the coming of the kingdom of God. The kingdom of God will overcome the power of sin in the world; love will prevail over division among people and division among spouses. "Jesus' word is therefore no crushing law," the three bishops write, "but rather an offer, an invitation, an exhortation and a gift, which is to realize the original sense of marriage in lifelong fidelity." Despite the teaching of Jesus, the church's experience from the beginning of its history shows that the power of sin has continued to be effective even among the baptized. This does not mean that the church can shut its eyes to the ideals expressed in the gospel, but equally it cannot shut its eyes to the failure of many marriages. The challenge of Jesus' words on marriage must be balanced with his command to love, to forgive and to show mercy.

The bishops continue this balanced approach in the next section on the responsibility of the Christian community. They state forcefully that Christians must oppose any trend that would regard divorce and remarriage as the norm or as a right. This would betray the message of Jesus. "However, the church must offer solidarity to those who have failed in marriage and who have decided upon a second, civil marriage." All Christians must avoid hardness and intransigence and must strive to make the divorced and remarried feel that the church is truly a healing and helping community.

In the following section, on participation in the sacraments, the bishops begin by noting that there are various grades and forms of participation in the church depending on the individual's situation in life and level of faith. While it is not possible to establish a general rule that all divorced and remarried Catholics may be admitted to the sacraments of penance and the eucharist, "it ought to be clarified through pastoral dialogue whether that which is generally valid applies also in a given situation." In other words, the three German bishops uphold as a general rule the traditional teaching that divorced and remarried persons are to be excluded from the sacraments; but they admit, in accord with standard principles of moral theology such as *epikeia,* that there can be exceptions to this rule in individual cases.

Following the pastoral letter, the three bishops provide principles of pastoral care for Catholic divorced persons. The foundational principle is that divorced and remarried people "are at home in the church and are inside the community of the church even though they are to some extent restricted with regard to some of the rights of all church members. They belong to us." On this point the bishops recall the teaching of Pope John Paul II in *Familiaris consortio,* written after the 1980 synod of bishops on the family: "Together with the synod, I earnestly call upon pastors and the whole community of the faithful to help the divorced and with solicitous care to make sure that they do not consider themselves as separated from the church, for as baptized persons they can and indeed must share in her life" (84).

Regarding sharing in the eucharist, the bishops restate the principle enunciated in *Familiaris consortio,* 84, which states that the divorced and remarried cannot be admitted to the sacrament because "their state and position in life objectively contradict that union of love between Christ and the church that is signified and effected by the eucharist." But they note, in addition, that the church has long granted admission to the sacraments to divorced and remarried persons who agree to abstain from sexual relations. This was also taught by Pope John Paul II. However, the bishops openly admit the fact that the brother-sister solution is considered by many today as "unnatural and unbelievable." While the bishops laud those Catholic couples in this situation who have chosen a life of continence, they realize that this ideal "cannot be achieved by all people who are divorced and remarried and only seldom by younger couples."

Without further development of this issue, the bishops go on to enunciate the criteria for discerning whether a divorced and remarried person can be admitted to the sacraments. The criteria are not new; they were developed by moral theologians years ago and have been refined in recent decades by professional boards of moral theologians and canonists, local church synods and pastoral committees. What is involved, in effect, is an examination of conscience by the divorced and remarried person, in dialogue with "a wise and experienced priest" who serves as confessor or spiritual adviser, that leads to a determination of whether the person has the suitable dispositions necesssary for admission to the sacraments. The criteria that must be examined in this process are as follows:

1. When there is serious failure involved in the break-up of the first marriage, responsibility for it must be acknowledged and there must be repentance.

2. It must be established that a return to the first partner is impossible and that the first marriage cannot be restored.

3. Restitution must be made for wrongs committed and injuries done, insofar as this is possible.

4. This restitution primarily requires fulfillment of obligations to the spouse and children of the first marriage.

5. There should be some consideration of whether or not a partner ended his or her first marriage under great public attention and possibly even scandal.

6. The second marital partnership must have proved itself over a long period of time to represent a publicly recognizable commitment to permanence and to the other demands of marriage.

7. It ought to be sufficiently clear — though certainly not to any greater extent than with other Christians — that the partners seek truly to live according to the Christian faith and with true motives, that is, that they are moved by genuinely religious desires to participate in the sacramental life of the church. The same holds true in the children's upbringing.

After an investigation of the circumstances of the first marriage and the problems that led to the divorce, and also after an examinination of the situation of the second marriage, persons in irregular marriages can be led to a responsible decision on whether their present state of life permits them in good conscience to approach the sacraments. The role of the priest is not to make that determination but to accompany the individual through the process of conversion that leads to a correct judgment. The priest does not pronounce any official judgment but is to respect the judgment of the individual as to whether he or she may in the eyes of God justifiably approach the eucharistic table.

There may not be any kind of ceremony or blessing of the second marriage. The internal forum solution affects only the individual's reception of the sacraments, especially the eucharist, and the second marriage remains invalid in the external forum. Catholic ministers may not officiate at a wedding ceremony or even at a mere blessing of an invalid marriage. A liturgical ceremony of whatever kind, the bishops state, "would not only lead to serious misunderstandings among many of the faithful regarding the indissolubility of a validly contracted Christian marriage but would also introduce official liturgical acts that create the impression of a new, sacramentally valid marriage."

Before concluding this discussion on the three German bishops' pastoral letter, a few further remarks on the internal forum solution should be made. Nearly all the literature on the internal forum solution reflects a traditional concern of the church that its use by divorced persons not cause any scandal in the community. Scandal could occur when persons in irregular unions receive the eucharist because it may seem to some that they are receiving unworthily and are disregarding the church's teaching. Those who counsel the internal forum solution should advise the person to receive communion in a church where no scandal will arise as a result of their doing so. This could even be the person's own parish — few North American Catholics are really scandalized anymore by divorced and remarried people receiving communion.

Due to the prevalence of annulments, the faithful are aware that the church has means to restore persons in irregular marriages to its sacramental life; and it is not assumed that they are receiving communion unworthily. On the contrary, a more common perception today is that the greater scandal lies in the church's refusal of the sacraments to those who have repented of the breakdown of their first marriage. Many Catholics do not understand why every sinner can be reconciled to the church, no matter how grievous the crime or the sin, with the exception of those who have remarried after a divorce, even if they were the innocent party to the failure of the first marriage.

Because it is possible according to traditional teaching for people in irregular unions to return to the sacraments by means of the internal forum solution, the minister of communion should not refuse the sacrament to them solely because their second marriage has not been regularized. Canon 915 of the *Code of Canon Law,* which states in part that those "who obstinately persist in manifest grave sin are not to be admitted to holy communion," does not apply automatically to all those in irregular marriages.[7] No minister should presume that such persons are always persisting in manifest grave sin.

The remainder of the pastoral principles attached to the letter of the three German bishops deals with other matters related to the place of divorced and remarried Catholics in the community and their pastoral care. An issue that sometimes arises is whether the divorced and remarried may be godparents. Although some pastors assume that the divorced and remarried may not act as godparents for baptism, the bishops point out that they are not to be automatically excluded but that in each case they are to be judged according to the same standard as others who wish to be godparents, in particular the requirement that they should be leading a life of faith in keeping with the role to be undertaken, as is required of any godparent (canon 874, 3°; CCEC canon 1240). Regarding the sacrament of anointing of the sick and Catholic funeral rites, the bishops urge that there be no unreasonable demands made in the case of the divorced and remarried. The bishops recall that all Catholics are required to have faith and the proper disposition to receive the sacraments; pastors should not make exceptional demands on the divorced and remarried that are not required of other faithful.

The CDF Letter

Although the pastoral letter of the three German bishops was intended only for the faithful in the three dioceses of the province of Upper Rhine, it received wide publicity and was translated into a number of languages. Other bishops made statements about it, some critical and negative, others supportive and grateful, still others expressed a "wait and see" stance. In December 1993, five months after the release of their letter to the people of their dioceses, the three bishops of the province of Upper Rhine received a letter from the Congregation for the Doctrine of the Faith informing them that they had not fully upheld Catholic teaching in their pastoral letter and attached principles. In February 1994, they went to Rome for a dialogue with the congregation. The German bishops believe that this discussion showed that their basic theological position was not contested in principle by the Holy See, but they did say that "no full agreement could be reached on the question of the reception of communion."[8] Further discussions were held in June. In September 1994, the CDF issued a letter to all bishops on the reception of communion by divorced and married Catholics.[9] Although the CDF made no mention of the German bishops' pastoral letter, it was widely considered the Vatican's response to the pastoral letter of the Upper Rhine dioceses.

The CDF letter repeats the traditional teaching of the church that the divorced and remarried may only receive communion if they are prepared to live a life of complete continence by abstaining from the sexual act and by avoiding scandal (n. 4). While acknowledging that a judgment about one's dispositions for the reception of holy communion must be made by a properly formed moral conscience, the letter recalls that "the consent that is the foundation of marriage is not simply a private decision since it creates a specifically ecclesial and social situation for the spouses, both individually and as a couple." The judgment involving one's own marital situation does not regard only the immediate relationship between the individual and God but also the mediation of the church, including its canonical discipline (8).

> The church is in fact the body of Christ, and to live in ecclesial communion is to live in the body of Christ and to nourish oneself with the body of Christ. With the reception of the sacrament of the eucharist, communion with Christ the head can never be separated from communion with his members, that is, with his church. For this reason, the sacrament of our union with Christ is also the sacrament of the unity of the church. Receiving eucharistic communion contrary to the norms of ecclesial communion is therefore in itself a contradiction (9).

The CDF upholds the importance of the individual's conscience, but it also notes that the sacraments of marriage and the eucharist are ecclesial acts that have ecclesial consequences. The sacraments are not simply for the benefit of an individual's private, spiritual relationship with God but involve other members of the Christian community. The reception of communion implies that the person is in communion with the church, including its teaching and discipline on who is eligible to receive communion. Personal conscience cannot go against the rules established by the church, according to the CDF. Since the church has established the rule that divorced and remarried persons may receive the sacraments only if they abstain from sexual relations, the internal forum solution is applicable only under this condition.

Response of the Three Bishops

Shortly after the CDF letter to the world's bishops, the three German bishops of the province of Upper Rhine issued their own response, once again addressing it to the faithful of their province.[10] They reiterated their agreement with the CDF on all fundamental points of doctrine. They continued to maintain their disagreement on the pastoral application of these doctrinal principles. In fact, in the second letter they argued their case more forcefully than they did the first time. The crux of the disagreement is whether the general rule, which prohibits the reception of the sacraments by the divorced and remarried, cannot be applied flexibly in individual cases.

The bishops argue that, according to standard principles of moral theology and canon law, a general rule must in each case be applied to concrete persons in their individual situations. The church's moral tradition has long recognized the virtue of *epikeia,* first formulated by Aristotle, whereby a general rule must be mitigated in particular cases where it is not fully applicable or where its observance would cause harm rather than good. A similar principle exists in canon law, the principle known as equity, which says that the law has to be applied with mercy as well as justice. The German bishops see these principles as applicable to the situation of the reception of the sacraments by the divorced and remarried. They maintain that the church's position barring persons in irregular marriages from reception of the sacraments is valid as a general rule but that this rule must be applied flexibly in pastoral practice, and with compassion and mercy, in accord with the varied situations of individuals.

Another point stressed by the bishops is the importance of individual conscience. They recall Vatican II's teaching on the role of conscience[11] and assert that the church's teaching cannot be convincing in the long run unless pastoral practice takes account of the very complex life situations of people and also of the individual's unique personal dignity as expressed in an educated conscience. A normative teaching or law cannot truly be appropriated by individuals unless it is mediated through their conscience. "The purer the conscience becomes," the bishops state, "the more it will be in a position to mediate the

141

demands of the divine order and to apply these to the concrete situation without distortion."

The bishops conclude by saying that they will continue, in dialogue with the faithful of their dioceses, to endeavor to come up with answers to this problem that are capable of generating a consensus and that are theologically and pastorally responsible. They encourage their people not to be critical and negative about the CDF letter but "to seek responsible solutions for individual cases in fidelity to the message of Jesus and the faith of the church as well as in solidarity with the people involved and in communion with the entire church." They end on a hopeful note, confident that their clergy and other ministers will act in a pastorally responsible way and give good advice to people in the light of the principles they set forth in their letter.

Further Considerations

The internal forum solution may still be used. What is in dispute is whether a person in an irregular marriage may return to the sacraments without giving up sexual relations with his or her spouse. According to the newer approaches, this brother-sister arrangement is not required; according to Pope John Paul II and the CDF, it is. Obviously, the universal magisterium of the church prevails because it is a higher authority than that of bishops acting in their own dioceses or regions. The new approaches to the internal forum solution that permit continued sexual relations between the parties to an irregular union have not been given the approbation of the Holy See. However, the German bishops expressed their wish that the discussion continue so that responsible solutions can be found that will assist divorced and remarried persons in returning to full participation in the life of the church but will also be faithful to the teachings of Jesus. It is in this same spirit of respectful searching that the following comments and questions are offered.

Divorce is rampant in modern society, and some segments of popular culture accept divorce and remarriage as perfectly

normal and acceptable. The Holy See has repeatedly taken
a countercultural stance against this divorce mentality and has
consistently upheld the value of permanence and stability in
marriage. Quite likely the reluctance of the Holy See to change
any part of its discipline regarding divorced and remarried
Catholics is due, at least in part, to a "political" desire to avoid
the public impression that it is permissive about divorce. However, this is not the full story. More fundamentally, in maintaining the brother-sister solution, the Holy See doubtless sees
itself in continuity with the gospel as it has come to be interpreted in Catholic tradition. There are two key questions that should
be at the heart of scholarly and pastoral reflection: Is the official
Roman Catholic interpretation of Jesus' teaching the only possible one? If not, is it possible for the church to change its
practice based on a different understanding of Jesus' teaching?

The teaching that is not in question here is the indissolubility
of marriage. The Catholic church has consistently believed
and taught that Christian marriage, by divine law, is to be permanent, dissolved only by death. The church permits the dissolution
only of non-sacramental marriages, when one or both parties
to the marriage were unbaptized, or of sacramental marriages
that have not been consummated by sexual intercourse. A
dissolution of a sacramental, consummated marriage is not given
and is considered impossible.[12]

The question at issue here is how the church should treat
its members who have sinned against the law of Christ by
remarrying after civil divorce without an annulment. Have they
committed the only unforgiveable sin? Should they be excluded
permanently from the sacraments and marginalized in the
eucharistic assembly? If they are unable to obtain an annulment,
is their restoration to full participation in the eucharist possible
only if they agree not to have sexual relations with their new
spouses? Are they committing adultery if they continue to have
sexual relations?

In the synoptic gospels, Jesus says that those who divorce
and marry another or marry someone divorced commit adultery.[13]
How should this teaching be interpreted? Is it to be taken as
an absolute norm applicable in every case at all times, or was
Jesus speaking of the general rule? The interpretation given

by most non-Catholic Christian churches is the latter.[14] They say that Jesus taught the indissolubility of marriage as the norm, the rule toward which all Christian married persons should strive, and he underlined the seriousness of this rule by saying that those who divorce and marry another commit adultery. However, Jesus consistently taught that those who sin against God's laws can be forgiven if they are repentant. God's mercy is extended to all sinners; no category of sinner is excluded.

It could well be objected that this interpretation waters down the words of Jesus. Perhaps it does; perhaps it does not. It is widely known that not everything Jesus said was meant to be taken literally. He often said outlandish things that startled his listeners, that forced them to take note and grapple with his message. Jesus taught in stories and parables, and like any good storyteller or teacher, he spoke in ways that would get peoples' attention and make them remember the core of his message. For example, in Matthew 5:29 – 30, just before his teaching on marriage, Jesus says: "If your right eye should cause you to sin, tear it out and throw it away. . . . And if your right hand should cause you to sin, cut it off and throw it away."[15] Christian tradition has not taken these words literally. In fact, the church has consistently taught the opposite, that self-mutilation is a mortal sin; in canon law, it is an irregularity that permanently prohibits a man from the reception of holy orders (canon 1041, 5°; CCEC 762, 5°). Everyone recognizes that plucking out one's eye or cutting off one's hand are exaggerations used to make the point that the followers of Jesus must try to avoid temptation and sin to the best of their ability.

These verses do not appear before the teaching on marriage in Mark and Luke, but the point is still valid that Jesus' words about adultery may not have been the core message he was trying to convey. Rather, it is quite possible that the real teaching is not about adultery at all but about the permanence of marriage, not that those who violate his command are perpetual adulterers but that they sin by remarrying and must do penance like other sinners. Jesus' words in the synoptic gospels, if taken to mean that divorced and remarried persons are perpetual sinners, would be uncharacteristic of his overall message of love, compassion and forgiveness. Might the better interpretation of Jesus' words be that indissolubility is the ideal to which every Christian married couple must strive daily to realize but that divorce and remarriage, like other sins, may be forgiven — that no one who repents is separated from God's mercy?

But does true repentance require abstinence from sexual relations? Numerous Catholic pastors, canonists and theologians do not think so. They consider such a "solution" to be unnatural and counterproductive. A married couple are not brother and sister, and "nature does not tolerate false pretenses. The natural dynamics, physical and psychological, between a brother and sister are unique and different from any other relationship between a man and a woman."[16] The importance of a healthy sex life in marriage is well known today, especially in the early years of marriage. Sexual intercourse in the marriage deepens love and fosters fidelity and permanence. When a couple is in a second marriage that is stable and characterized by love and fidelity, what pastor would want to risk having a successful union shattered by imposing the brother-sister solution on the couple?

Joseph Ratzinger, before he became prefect of the CDF, is an example of a mainstream Catholic appoach to the internal forum solution. His writings draw on teachings of the early fathers of the church and the church's moral tradition. In an essay published in 1972, he wrote:

> Whenever in a second marriage moral obligations have arisen toward the children, toward the family and toward the woman, and no similar obligations from the first marriage exist; whenever also the giving up of the second marriage is not permissible [not fitting] on moral grounds, and continence does not appear as a real possibility in the practical order; it seems that the granting of full communion, after a time of probation, is nothing less than just, and is fully in harmony with our ecclesiastical traditions. The concession of communion in such a case cannot depend on an act that would be either immoral or factually impossible.[17]

For many couples, especially younger couples, complete abstinence from sexual relations may be a practical impossibility. Ratzinger indicated it could be immoral if it led to the destruction of their union, in which there are obligations to one another and to children. What pastor of the church would urge the brother-sister solution at the risk of producing an immoral result?

Ratzinger's views come from the best tradition of Catholic moral theology. He upholds the indissolubility of marriage but is also understanding of the reality of human need: "Marriage is a sacrament," he says; "it consists of an unbreakable structure, created by a firm decision. But this should not exclude the grant of ecclesial communion to those persons who acknowledge this teaching as a principle of life but find themselves in an emergency situation of a specific kind, in which they have a particular need to be in communion with the body of the Lord."[18]

Another reason scholars suggest for discarding the brother-sister solution is that it makes no sense in view of the theology of marriage taught by the Second Vatican Council. Before the council, church teaching on marriage was heavily juridical in its approach, emphasizing the nature of marriage as a legal contract by which the parties exchanged with each other the "right to the body," the right to sexual intercourse (1917 CIC, canon 1081). Once this contract was consummated by sexual intercourse, a juridical bond was formed that could not be broken, even after divorce and remarriage.

Vatican II, by contrast, did not say that marriage was a contract. It spoke of marriage in biblical and theological language, calling it a covenant and an intimate partnership of life and love.[19] The conciliar theology of marriage is expressed in canon 1055 of the 1983 code, the initial canon in the section on marriage. Here marriage is defined as a covenant by which a man and a woman establish between themselves a "partnership of the whole of life" *(consortium totius vitae)*. Under the former law, when marriage was considered a contract granting the partners the right to sexual relations, the brother-sister solution made sense, at least according to the juridical theory, because in that arrangement the right of the previous spouse was not violated so long as the couple in the second marriage abstained from sexual intercourse. However, when marriage is viewed as a *consortium,* a partnership of the whole life and an intimate communion of life and love, the brother-sister arrangement cannot uphold the rights and obligations of the previous valid union. On the contrary, the element of love and support of the couple in the second union is urged as an essential component of the brother-sister arrangement. Only those in such a stable, loving, caring union have been said to qualify for the brother-sister solution.

Another argument that has been proposed against the brother-sister solution is one that compares divorced and remarried Catholics with non-Catholic Christians. The CDF explains in its letter that it is not possible for divorced and remarried persons to share in the eucharist because reception of the eucharist requires communion with the church. This is the same reason Protestants ordinarily may not receive the sacraments from Catholic ministers, especially the eucharist. Full participation in the eucharist is a sign of full communion with the church. However, canon 844 permits non-Catholic Christians to receive Catholic sacraments in special situations of spiritual need. The parallel with divorced and remarried Catholics is evident. They are excluded from the sacraments as a general rule, as are Protestants. Should they also not be admitted to the sacraments in individual cases of spiritual need?

If a reexamination of the Catholic position that equates remarriage with adultery would some day recommend a revision of this position, it would also be necessary to determine whether the church has the power to make such a revision. When the Roman see determines that some matter cannot be changed, not infrequently it does so out of the conviction that, in fidelity to the scriptures and tradition, it lacks the power to change what has always been, and what might be of divine law. To what extent does or does not the church have the power to change its traditional interpretation of Jesus' teaching? His teaching itself cannot change, but human, fallible interpretations can. And it is only the church that has the power to interpret authoritatively the meaning of the scriptures and the truths of the faith. Only the church can do this, because the church is the living body of Christ throughout history to which Christ himself has given the power of the keys (Matthew 16:19).

The Latin church has long held that there is a special power granted uniquely to Peter and his successors, the popes. This power was used, for example, in the development of the "Petrine privilege," by which a marriage between a Christian and a non-baptized may be dissolved in favor of the faith. The most significant development of the privilege came about as recently as 1924 in the famous Helena case. Of this case, John T. Noonan Jr. writes:

> Prior to 1924 the teaching of the church, expressly grounded on both the commandment of the Lord and on the natural law, was that marriage was indissoluble except in the special case of conversion of an unbeliever [the Pauline privilege]. The teaching was unanimously expressed by papal encyclicals and by the body of bishops in their universal ordinary teaching. Then, in 1924, by the exercise of papal authority, the meaning of the commandment against adultery was altered; what was bigamy was revised; and a substantial gloss was written on the Lord's words, "What God has joined together let no man put asunder."[20]

The change in church practice in 1924 was far more momentous than the change being debated here. Here it is not a question of dissolving a marriage or of recognizing the legitimacy of a second marriage but of only allowing repentant Catholics to return to the sacraments. Who would want to deny that the Supreme Pontiff lacks the power to permit this?

The Orthodox churches recognize that all bishops possess a special power inherent in the practice of *oikonomia*. This is a mysterious power, not capable of canonical definition, that is an imitation of God's mercy, a prudent exercise of church stewardship by the bishop. It aims for the general well-being of the Christian community and of each individual, but it cannot be used contrary to dogma. Its purpose is to avoid the severity of the law, to eliminate the obstacles to salvation caused by rigid, legalistic interpretation.[21] From ancient times until now, Eastern bishops have used the power of *oikonomia* to heal persons who have suffered broken marriages.[22]

The bishops of the 1980 synod called for a thorough investigation of the Eastern practice in the hope that a compassionate solution could be found for divorced and remarried persons.[23] The concept of *oikonomia* is most promising. This power has been repeatedly exercised in the Orthodox churches over many centuries; it exists no less in the Catholic churches. It is inconceivable that Christ would give a power to the Orthodox bishops and withhold it from Catholics. Catholic bishops implicitly possess this power, but they have little or no understanding of it and no tradition for its exercise. Might the Eastern practice assist the Roman Catholic church to come to a solution that is faithful to Christ's command yet also compassionate and merciful?

The church cannot change the divine law. Because the church understands that the doctrine of indissolubility is divine law, it cannot accept civil divorce as the termination of marriage. But that does not mean that no revision of the church's position is possible. Under the guidance of the Holy Spirit, the church from time to time has changed its teaching on other moral issues, such as the morality of slavery, which was once acceptable but is no longer; usury, which was once condemned but for centuries now has been accepted; and religious freedom, which for centuries was denied to be a right only to be conceded as such at Vatican II.[24] Even today, there is evidence of a shift in teaching on an important moral issue. A consensus is growing among Catholic authorities that capital punishment can no longer be morally considered a legitimate option as it once was; tolerating the execution of offenders is inconsistent with the church's pro-life ethic and compromises its stance against abortion.

The church has the authority to revise the way it expresses the truth of doctrinal and moral questions in light of new understandings. In fact, the teaching of Jesus on divorce has been reinterpreted repeatedly, beginning in the New Testament itself. Mark, Matthew and Paul each interpolated Christ's teaching on divorce to respond to the needs and circumstances of their own particular audiences. Post-apostolic churches did the same.[25] New situations in human history and culture may give rise to changes in the church's understanding of complex moral issues. The Spirit-filled church of Christ may reach new insights in one age that were not relevant to an earlier age or were not comprehended by it.

Conclusion

The problem of divorce is not going away. Catholic marriages end in divorce at the same rate as non-Catholic marriages.

Scholarly research and pastoral discussion should continue to explore the most fitting ways that the church can extend Christ's healing love and mercy to divorced persons, including those in subsequent, irregular marriages. The hope cannot be extinguished that such study will someday enable those divorced and remarried Catholics who earnestly desire to practice their faith fully to approach the Lord's table with a clear conscience and with the disposition proper to all communicants, who pray: "Lord, I am not worthy to receive you, but only say the word and I shall be healed."

NOTES

[1]Matthew 19:6; Mark 10:9. The technical term "irregular union" includes not only divorced and remarried persons but also those who were not previously married and who marry a divorced person. However, we will use the non-technical term "divorced and remarried" to include both cases since this is the more common usage.

[2]November 21, 1981, AAS 74 (1982): 81–191, n. 84; *Origins* 11 (1981): 465.

[3]December 4, 1984, AAS 77 (1985): 185–275, n. 34; *Origins* 14 (1984): 454.

[4]See James H. Provost, "Intolerable Marriage Situations Revisited," *The Jurist* 40 (1980): 141–96. Kenneth R. Himes and James A. Coriden, "Pastoral Care of the Divorced and Remarried," *Theological Studies* 57 (1996): 97–123. See also *Ministering to the Divorced Catholic,* ed. James Young (New York: Paulist, 1979).

[5]See, for example, Geoffrey Robinson, *Marriage, Divorce & Nullity: A Guide to the Annulment Process in the Catholic Church* (Collegeville: Liturgical Press, 1987); Joseph Zwack, *Annulment: Your Chance to Remarry Within the Catholic Church* (Cambridge: Harper & Row, 1983); Terrence E. Tierney and Joseph J. Campo, *Annulment: Do You Have a Case?,* 2nd ed. revised and updated (New York: Alba House, 1993).

[6]Joint pastoral letter, July 10, 1993; translation in *Origins* 23 (1994): 674.

[7]CCEC canon 712 states: "Those who are publicly unworthy are to be prevented from receiving the divine eucharist."

For an excellent study of the canonical issues, see Patrick J. Travers, "Reception of the Holy Eucharist by Catholics Attempting Remarriage After Divorce and the 1983 Code of Canon Law," *The Jurist* 55 (1995): 187–217. Since canon law does not exclude all divorced and remarried from the sacraments, Travers makes the important point that the teaching of the CDF has to be harmonized with the law because the issue of a fundamental right to the sacraments is involved. See canons 213 and 912.

[8]"Response to the Vatican Letter," *Origins* 24 (1994): 342.

[9]September 14, 1994, *Origins* 24 (1994): 337–41.

[10]Citation at note 8, pp. 341–44.

[11]Declaration on Religious Liberty, *Dignitatis humanae,* 3.

[12]There is possibility for further theological and canonical developments on the church's understanding of "consummation in a human manner." Is it merely the mutually free act of sexual intercourse after marriage, or is it, as has been suggested, the establishment of the marital consortium? If the latter, then the competent ecclesiastical authority could dissolve sacramental marriages in which the couple has failed to develop an intimate partnership of conjugal life and love. This is argued in Michael G. Lawler, "Blessed are Spouses who Love, for their Marriages will be Permanent: A Theology of the Bonds of Marriage," *The Jurist* 55 (1995): 218–242.

[13]Mark 10:11–12; Matthew 5:32; Luke 16:18. The wording and context of each differ in significant respects.

[14]For the Orthodox position, see John Meyendorff, *Marriage: An Orthodox Perspective* (Crestwood, NY: St. Vladimir, 1975).

[15]Translation from *The Jerusalem Bible* (London: Darton, Longman and Todd, 1966).

[16]Ladislas Örsy, *Marriage in Canon Law* (Wilmington, Delaware: Michael Glazier, 1986): 291.

[17]"Zur Frage nach der Unauflösigkeit der Ehe," in *Ehe und Ehescheidung* (München: Kösel, 1972) 55; translation in Örsy, 292.

[18]Ibid., 55–56; Örsy, 293.

[19]The Pastoral Constitution on the Church in the Modern World, *Gaudium et spes,* 48.

[20]Noonan, "Development in Moral Doctrine," *Theological Studies* 54 (1993): 662–77.

[21]"Oikonomia," *The Oxford Dictionary of Byzantium* (New York: Oxford University, 1991): 1516. See also Ladislas Örsy, *Theology and Canon Law* (Collegeville: Liturgical Press, 1992): 73–74.

[22]*The Oxford Dictionary of Byzantium,* 640.

[23]Proposition 14, n. 6, *Enchiridion Vaticanum* 7, 2nd ed. (Bologna: 1990): 688, n. 729.

[24]Noonan, 662–77.

[25]For a thorough study, see Theodore Mackin, *Marriage in the Catholic Church: Divorce and Remarriage* (New York/Ramsey: Paulist, 1984).

Eucharistic Reservation

Questions about eucharistic reservation arise frequently today. When a church is being built or renovated, a common source of conflict is where to put the tabernacle. The ideas of liturgical consultants are sometimes met with resistance by parishioners and opposed by the bishop himself. Other questions arise regarding the personal retention of the eucharist, with deacons and lay ministers of the eucharist needing access to the sacrament for the exercise of their ministry. There are also doubts about how to respond to requests by small groups of people, or even individuals, who wish to reserve the eucharist solely for the purpose of adoration. The laws of the church in the code and in the liturgical books have evolved on this matter since Vatican ii, and these changes have caused some of the confusion. But a close look at this legislative evolution will reveal consistent principles that should resolve most conflicts on questions of eucharistic reservation.

The first part of this essay addresses the question of the proper place for eucharistic reservation in churches and oratories. The second part considers eucharistic reservation in special circumstances.

The Proper Place

In most churches prior to Vatican II, there was no question of how the blessed sacrament was to be reserved. Canon 1268 of the 1917 *Code of Canon Law* established the general rule that the tabernacle was to be affixed to the center of the main altar of the church. Now the rule is the opposite. It ought *not* be reserved on the main altar, and several options are possible. A brief historical review will show that the current options are more faithful to the variety of practices that existed for many centuries.

The practice of reserving some of the consecrated bread and/or wine after the celebration of Mass originated in the ancient church for the purpose of sharing holy communion with those who could not participate with the community at the Sunday eucharistic celebration.[1] This included the sick and dying, those in hiding during times of persecution, and other persons who might have been absent from the celebration. There was no appointed place for reservation. Frequently the eucharist was kept in the priest's house, and in some places the faithful even took the eucharist home to receive communion during the week. By the early Middle Ages, evidence increasingly suggests, the sacristy or similar room adjacent to the church was the ordinary place of reservation.

Gradually this area of the church's life, like many others, became subject to ecclesiastical legislation. By the end of the ninth century, regulations in some areas directed that the eucharist be reserved within the church itself in close proximity to the altar; but there was still no uniform legislation. The sacred bread was variously kept in a small box *(arca),* a wicker basket, an ornate container called a chrismal, a dove-shaped container, a small movable tower, a pyx or an ambry in the wall.

By the thirteenth century it had become more common, though by no means generally required, to reserve the eucharist on or over the altar. The earliest tabernacles were built onto the wall. In the seventeenth century, a tabernacle positioned on the main altar became commonplace in the West and this custom later became the general law.

Blessed Sacrament Chapel

This brief survey reveals a wide variety in the course of church history of places and means for reserving the eucharist. Some variety still exists in law and custom today. The place most favored for eucharistic reservation by the law is a tabernacle placed in a separate blessed sacrament chapel adjacent to the church (GIRM, 276; HCW, 9). As a rule, there can be only one tabernacle in each church (canon 938, §1; GIRM, 277; HCW, 10). The preference for placing the tabernacle in a separate chapel was originally expressed in the 1967 instruction on the worship of the eucharistic mystery, *Eucharisticum mysterium*.[2] The instruction stated that the place where the eucharist is reserved should be suitable for private prayer and therefore in a chapel separated from the central nave of the church, especially in those churches where marriages or funerals occur frequently and in those places that are visited by many people because of artistic and historic treasures.

The Bishops' Committee on the Liturgy of the United States episcopal conference gives an important theological motive for the primacy of a separate chapel for eucharistic reservation: "A room or chapel specifically designed and separate from the major space is important so that no confusion can take place between the celebration of the eucharist and reservation. Active and static aspects of the same reality cannot claim the same human attention at the same time."[3] The eucharistic celebration and the reserved sacrament are two different aspects of Christ's eucharistic presence; one is active, the other static. The focus of the assembly gathered for the celebration of the eucharist should be on the active presence of Christ in all its modes: in the assembly and its ministers, in the proclamation of the word and in the breaking of the bread. When the tabernacle is visually proximate to the altar, the focus on the sacramental action can be obscured.

Wall Niche, Pillar, Tower

If it is impossible to reserve the eucharist in a separate room or chapel, the tabernacle is preferably placed in the church in a wall niche or on a pillar, or reserved in a eucharistic tower. The tabernacle should not be placed on an altar, because the altar is a place for action, not for reservation. The options of the wall niche, pillar and eucharistic tower are given in the BCL document *Environment and Art in Catholic Worship*. This document is not liturgical law properly so called. Nevertheless, the options it gives are rooted in the church's history and are in accord with the universal law. The legitimacy of these options follows from the law of the Roman Pontifical, which says that there should be only one altar in new churches.[4]

The law prefers only one altar in a church, and the tabernacle may not be placed on this main altar. If there is no blessed sacrament chapel, then it follows that the tabernacle should be placed somewhere else besides an altar (since ideally there should be only one altar). Therefore the tabernacle must be located in some other place legitimated by tradition, such as in a wall niche or on a pillar. The eucharist may also be reserved in a tower that can be built in such a way that it serves as the tabernacle itself. The law requires that the tabernacle be immovable, made of solid and opaque material, and locked to prevent desecration (canon 938, §3; HCW, 10; GIRM, 277).

Sufficient hosts are to be kept in the tabernacle for the needs of the faithful who must communicate outside Mass, especially the sick and the dying. These hosts should be renewed frequently (canon 939); fresh breads are to be consecrated at each eucharistic celebration for the communion of the assembly (HCW, 13). The Secretariat of the BCL correctly observes that "the practice of using mostly hosts that are reserved in the tabernacle for distribution at Mass or, worse yet, only consecrating a host for the priest-celebrant are evidently contrary to the liturgical books."[5]

Tabernacle on a Side Altar

Eucharisticum mysterium, 10 permitted a small tabernacle to
be placed on the main altar but clearly did not favor this practice: "From the viewpoint of sign, it is more in keeping with the
nature of the sacred celebration that the eucharistic presence of
Christ, which is the result of the consecration and must appear to
be such, should not be found at the altar where Mass is celebrated, if it can be avoided, from the beginning of Mass through
reservation of the holy species in the tabernacle" (DOL 1239).
This 1967 instruction can be seen as a transitional document
moving away from the practice of placing the tabernacle on the
altar, without actually forbidding it, to the preferred practice
of having a blessed sacrament chapel or exercising some other
option. The intent of the current law is clear: The tabernacle
should not be placed on the main altar. The *General Instruction
of the Roman Missal,* 276 nevertheless mentions an altar as an
option for the tabernacle when it is impossible to have a blessed
sacrament chapel. However, this norm was published many
years ago in 1969, and it is not a good indicator of the current
position of the Holy See on this issue. It should now be understood to mean a side altar, not the main altar.

In 1983 the Holy See dropped from the Roman Ritual the
express mention of an altar as a possible place for the tabernacle.[6]
This suggests that the legislator no longer includes the altar
as an option for the place of reservation. This does not mean that
the placement of the tabernacle on a side altar is forbidden; as
seen above, the provision for this is still found in the *General
Instruction of the Roman Missal.* Rather, its elimination from the
Roman Ritual in 1983 suggests that the placement of the tabernacle on a side altar is, all things being equal, the least preferred
of the options. However, all things sometimes are not equal.
Limited financial means or a restricted architectural space may
sometimes dictate that the side altar is the more appropriate
place for the tabernacle. For example, when the sanctuary is
narrow, it may be preferable to reserve the eucharist on a side
altar rather than have the tabernacle placed too close to the main

157

altar, where the primary focus on the eucharistic action would be obscured. An even better solution in this case would be to remove the side altar and reserve the eucharist in that space in a wall niche, on a pillar or in a tower. This would be feasible in most North American churches, where side altars lack significant artistic or historical value.

In many places the tabernacle still has not been removed from the old main altar, which is situated directly behind the altar of celebration. From what has been said above, it is evident that this is not a satisfactory situation. Unless the tabernacle has significant artistic value and cannot be moved from the old main altar without damaging the church's architectural integrity, then the pastor or rector should begin to explore other alternatives. As in all substantive matters of art and environment affecting public worship spaces, decisions on the place for eucharistic reservation should be made in consultation with a good architect and a liturgical consultant.[7]

The second part of this essay will apply the law on eucharistic reservation to some special cases that have arisen in various places in North America. But first it may be helpful to summarize the provisions of law as already discussed.

1. The clear preference of church law is that the eucharist be reserved not in the main body of the church but in a separate chapel or room suitable for private devotion. If there is a blessed sacrament chapel, the eucharist may only be reserved there; it may not also be reserved in the church.

2. If there is no separate chapel or room, the preferred options are to reserve the eucharist in a tabernacle positioned in a wall niche or on a pillar, or to reserve it in a eucharistic tower. It should be located away from the action of the eucharistic celebration at the main altar.

3. The law prefers that there be only one altar in the church. In older churches that still have side altars, one of them may be used for eucharistic reservation when there is no other suitable place for the tabernacle away from the main altar. A better solution would be to replace the side altar with a wall niche, pillar or eucharistic tower.

4. It is preferable not to reserve the eucharist on the old main altar behind the altar of celebration unless there are serious artistic reasons for doing so.

5. The tabernacle should not be placed on the altar used for the eucharistic celebration.

Eucharistic Reservation in Special Circumstances

In recent years new questions about the proper place of eucharistic reservation have arisen out of new situations in the contemporary church. For example, small religious communities consisting of several members living in a house or apartment sometimes want to have the eucharist reserved there. Another example is deacons or lay eucharistic ministers who want to keep the eucharist in their house overnight or during the week so that they might more conveniently exercise their ministry. Is eucharistic reservation justifiable and lawful in such circumstances?

Canons 934 and 936 of the *Code of Canon Law* establish some basic rules on the place of eucharistic reservation. (1) The eucharist *must* be reserved in all cathedrals and parish churches and in the church or oratory attached to the house of a religious institute or society of apostolic life. (2) Although not mandatory, the eucharist *can* be reserved in the private chapel of a bishop and, with permission of the local ordinary, in other churches (such as shrines), oratories or chapels. In religious houses, the eucharist is to be reserved in the principal church or oratory; but for a just cause, the ordinary can permit reservation in another oratory of the same house. In any sacred place where the eucharist is reserved, a priest must celebrate Mass there at least twice a month, insofar as this is possible.

The proper place for eucharistic reservation is therefore a sacred place where the eucharist is regularly celebrated. A principal reason for this rule is to uphold the intimate connection between the celebration of the eucharist and its reservation. Christ instituted the eucharist as an action — a meal, an offering of thanks and praise, a sharing of his body and blood in holy communion. Nevertheless, from early times Christian communities have kept some of the bread and/or wine blessed at the

159

Sunday assembly for the purpose of taking it to those who could not be present due to infirmity or persecution; thus they too could have a share in the sacred meal.

The purposes for eucharistic reservation are prioritized in the Roman Ritual: "The primary and original reason for reservation of the eucharist outside Mass is the administration of viaticum. The secondary reasons are the giving of communion and the adoration of our Lord Jesus Christ who is present in the sacrament" (HCW, 5). Eucharistic adoration and communion outside Mass are secondary reasons for reservation; viaticum for the dying is primary. Accordingly, canon law requires eucharistic reservation in cathedrals, parish churches and churches and oratories of religious institutes and societies of apostolic life, all of which must be prepared for the pastoral care of the sick and the dying.

Although adoration is a secondary reason for reservation, it is a practice highly commended by the church. In the course of history, eucharistic devotions arose due to the growing consciousness of the church that special honor is to be given to the abiding presence of Christ in the eucharistic elements reserved for viaticum and communion outside Mass. Adoration of the eucharist follows from reservation. The church first reserved the eucharist for its members in special need; as a consequence of reservation, practices associated with eucharistic adoration arose later. The eucharist was not reserved in order to adore it but was adored because it was reserved.

Ordinarily, only the consecrated bread is reserved; but the law also permits the reservation of the precious blood in order to bring communion under both kinds or, in necessity, under the species of wine alone, to those who are sick or dying. The precious blood is not to be reserved for other purposes, although this would not be excluded in a case of necessity, for example, when too much wine has been inadvertently consecrated at one Mass and must be reserved for consumption at a later Mass.

Small Religious Communities

The laws governing eucharistic reservation are designed to
protect some important theological values. Cases of eucharistic
reservation outside of the sacred places established by law
must be evaluated in light of the law and the values it represents.
The first case we will consider is that of small religious communities who want eucharistic reservation in a house that does
not have a canonically established oratory or private chapel.

With the establishment of a canonically erected religious
house comes the legal right to have the eucharist reserved in the
church or oratory of that house. However, many religious in
the United States do not live in a house that has been formally
established in accord with the law. A true religious *domus*
(house) must have three essential elements: (1) it must be legitimately constituted by the competent authority of the institute
with the previous written consent of the diocesan bishop; (2) it
must be under the authority of the competent superior; and
(3) it must have a church or oratory in which the eucharist is
celebrated and reserved (canons 608, 609).

If any of these elements are lacking, the building in question
does not meet the legal requirements of a canonical *domus,*
and the religious who live there do not have a right to eucharistic
reservation. However, even when the religious do not live in a
canonical house, the local ordinary can give them permission to
have the eucharist reserved when two conditions are met:
(1) The house has a church or oratory that has been legitimately
erected, and (2) the eucharist is regularly celebrated in this
church or oratory.

First, the house in question must have a church or oratory
in order for the eucharist to be reserved there. The eucharist is
not to be reserved in a closet, spare room or multi-purpose
space. Churches and oratories are sacred places that have been
dedicated or blessed in accord with the liturgical rites and set
aside for the exercise or promotion of worship, piety or religion
(canons 1205, 1210). A *church* is a sacred place which the
faithful have the right to attend (for example, the parish church).
An *oratory* is a sacred place established for a community or

group of persons to which other members of the faithful may go with the permission of the competent superior (canons 1214, 1223).

The erection of a church requires the written consent of the diocesan bishop (canon 1215). The erection of an oratory requires the permission of the competent ordinary. An "ordinary" in canon law is a generic term that includes the diocesan bishop, vicar general and episcopal vicar, all of whom are "local" ordinaries. Ordinaries who are not local ordinaries are the major superiors of clerical religious institutes of pontifical right and of clerical societies of apostolic life of pontifical right (canon 134). If the religious community in question is lay, the local ordinary is the competent authority to grant the permission to establish an oratory. He may not grant permission to establish an oratory unless he personally inspects the place or is assured by someone he delegates that it is suitably constructed (canon 1224).

Second, provision must be made for the regular celebration of the eucharist in the church or oratory of reservation. The code establishes the general rule that this be at least twice a month insofar as possible (canon 934, §2). There is some flexibility in the law in cases where it is impossible to celebrate the eucharist at least twice a month, but this flexibility should not become an excuse for neglecting the rule altogether. The law upholds an important theological value, namely the maintenance of the intrinsic connection between the eucharist celebrated and reserved. Another value of the law is to ensure the frequent renewal of the hosts (canon 939).

The constitutions of some religious institutes require eucharistic reservation in their "houses," which should be understood as the church or oratory connected to their houses. This requirement, also found in canon law, pertains to all religious, not only those who may have a special devotion to the blessed sacrament. The constitutional norms in question must be interpreted in accord with the universal law discussed here, especially the law that the eucharist must be reserved in a proper church or oratory. The fact that the constitutions require eucharistic reservation cannot be used as a basis for permitting reservation outside a church or oratory.

Other Cases

A variety of other cases have surfaced in recent years. Some requests for eucharistic reservation have little or no merit and should not be permitted by the competent ordinary. For example, individual priests, religious, hermits or others may desire reservation in their homes for personal adoration. While adoration before the blessed sacrament is encouraged by the church, retention of the eucharist by private persons, even priests, is not permitted. Only bishops have the legal right to a private chapel with the same rights as an oratory (canon 1227), including the right to reserve the eucharist, but even bishops are obliged to observe the requirement that Mass be celebrated there at least twice a month.

The church's liturgy, especially its sacraments, are preeminently *ecclesial* actions. On this point canon 837 quotes directly from Vatican II's *Constitution on the Sacred Liturgy,* 26: "Liturgical actions are not private actions but celebrations of the church itself." The reserved eucharist, although not a sacramental celebration, maintains its connectedness to the eucharistic action through its reservation in a sacred place where Mass is celebrated by the Christian community. The reservation of the eucharist by private individuals merely for reasons of personal piety is at least an anomaly, if not an outright abuse, and should not be permitted. As noted above, reservation outside a sacred place is forbidden, even in a room of a rectory or convent. Individuals and small groups who request eucharistic reservation should be encouraged instead to make visits to the blessed sacrament in their parish church in accord with canon 937.

Other requests for eucharistic reservation may have more merit, especially if they are intended to facilitate the pastoral care of the sick and dying. As deacons and lay ministers increasingly assume regular pastoral duties once exercised by a priest living near the church, practical problems can arise regarding their access to the tabernacle in the parish church. In some remote areas, these ministers live many miles from the church and exercise their ministry throughout the week, not only after Mass or after another liturgical celebration on Sunday.

In order for private persons to retain the eucharist, canon law requires "urgent pastoral need" and the observance of the precepts of the diocesan bishop (canon 935). A precept, unlike a law, is not a general policy for the whole community but a command given to an individual or small group. This implies that the bishop or the liturgical commission (if mandated by him) ought to consider the individual merits of each case rather than issue general guidelines applicable to all eucharistic ministers. It must be a case of "urgent pastoral need," and there must be assurance that the blessed sacrament is kept in a place that is suitable and safe.

By way of summary, the principal provisions of canon law governing the proper place for eucharistic reservation are as follows:

1. The local ordinary may grant permission for the eucharist to be reserved only in a church, oratory or chapel that has been set aside exclusively for cultic and religious purposes. The local ordinary is not to grant this permission unless he is assured personally or through a delegate that the sacred place is suitable.

2. In every sacred place where the eucharist is reserved, Mass must be celebrated on a regular basis, at least twice a month, insofar as this is possible.

3. The diocesan bishop, in individual cases, may permit ministers of viaticum and holy communion to keep the eucharist in a suitable place outside the parish church when there is "urgent pastoral need."

These rules may appear to some well-intentioned faithful as unduly restrictive, but they serve to protect important values — not only the custody of the blessed sacrament but also theological values, especially the intimate connection between the celebration of the eucharist and the reserved eucharist and the ecclesial context for the eucharist. The eucharist should only be reserved in a sacred place where Mass is regularly celebrated, and it should not be kept in the possession of private persons, even priests, except when the diocesan bishop permits it for urgent pastoral reasons.

NOTES

[1]For a thorough study see Archdale A. King, *Eucharistic Reservation in the Western Church* (New York: Sheed and Ward, 1965).

[2]Congregation of Sacred Rites, May 25, 1967, n. 53; DOL 179.

[3]*Environment and Art in Catholic Worship,* 78 (Washington: USCC, 1978).

[4]Rite of Dedication of an Altar, 7.

[5]*Eucharistic Worship and Devotion Outside Mass,* Study Text 11 (Washington: USCC, 1987): 23.

[6]Formerly this provision was found in HCW, 10. For the revision, see *Emendations in the Liturgical Books Following upon the New Code of Canon Law* (Washington: USCC, 1984): 10.

[7]This is also a requirement of canon law; canon 1216 states: "The principles and norms of the liturgy and of sacred art are to be observed in the building and repair of churches; the advice of experts is also to be employed."

The Age for Confirmation

Few pastoral-liturgical questions in recent years have occasioned greater difference of opinion among segments of Latin-rite Catholics than the issue of the age for confirmation. Since the revised *Rite of Confirmation* was promulgated in 1971, and even before that in some places, the trend has been to delay confirmation beyond the canonical age of seven. The rationale for this delay is the theological position that holds that confirmation is a "sacrament of spiritual maturity" whose recipients must be able to make a mature commitment to the faith of their baptism, which they received as infants. As a result, the age for confirmation in North America now varies from diocese to diocese and within some dioceses from parish to parish. The actual age often seems quite arbitrarily chosen on the basis of what someone in authority believes to be the age when a mature commitment is possible.

Despite the prevailing trend toward a higher age for confirmation, in more recent years religious educators and pastoral ministers in increasing numbers have been persuaded to adopt a quite different view of confirmation. The scholarship of liturgists and others has demonstrated to them that the significance of this second sacrament of Christian life is best disclosed when it is celebrated together with baptism and eucharist, the other sacraments of initiation. Hence, an effort is being made in some parishes and dioceses to try to restore the original, proper and authentic sequence of Christian initiation by celebrating confirmation immediately after baptism or, in the case of those baptized as infants, immediately before the reception of first communion.

This essay will consider several reasons why experts today by and large favor an earlier, rather than a later, age for the confirmation of those who were baptized as infants. Relevant laws from the *Code of Canon Law* and the liturgical books will be cited to establish what is legally permissible and desirable regarding the age for confirmation in the Latin church. To contextualize this treatment there will first be a brief overview of some aspects of the complex history of confirmation. This will bring out the sacrament's ritual and theological relatedness to baptism and eucharist.[1] A few remarks in relation to this discussion will also be made on the minister of confirmation.

Historical-Theological Context

According to the common consensus of scholars today, the early tradition of the church does not witness to a separate rite of confirmation apart from baptism but rather points to a unified initiation rite that included the elements of washing with water, imposition of hands (in some traditions), anointing with oil and completion of initiation with full participation in the eucharist. Infants who were baptized were also confirmed and received communion; indeed, infant communion did not die out in the West until about 1200 and is still practiced in Eastern churches.

In the early centuries, the postbaptismal anointing with the oil blessed by the bishop was so much an integral part of the initiation ritual that it was not perceived to be a separate sacrament. The initiation liturgies in most areas contained only one postbaptismal anointing, which was administered either by the bishop or by a presbyter. This is still the practice in Eastern churches today and the practice in the Latin church at the initiation of those seven and older according to the *Rite of Christian Initiation of Adults* (RCIA).

The original minister of all the sacraments was the bishop, but as the church began to grow and dioceses spread out to rural areas, it became impossible for the bishop to preside everywhere. So presbyters also began to celebrate the sacraments. In most places, presbyters performed the full rite of initiation, including the postbaptismal rituals which later came to be called confirmation.

An exception was the initiatory pattern of the diocese of Rome and the neighboring areas that followed the Roman practice. There, the imposition of hands and the anointing on the forehead were reserved to the bishop; thus they were delayed until it was possible for the bishop to be present when baptism was administered by a presbyter or deacon. This Roman pattern of splitting the initiation rite into separate rites performed by separate ministers became predominant in the Western church after the Carolingian reforms of the eighth and ninth centuries. Liturgists refer to this medieval development as the "disintegration" or "degeneration" of sacramental initiation.

Early in the twentieth century, Pope Pius x combated the Jansenistic influence over pastoral practice and religious education in many countries. This rigoristic spirituality held that most people were unworthy to receive communion frequently and that children had to prove themselves worthy for first holy communion through an extended catechetical program up to the age of ten, twelve, fourteen or older. The pope responded by standardizing the age for the reception of first communion and first penance at seven.[2] Confirmation was still supposed to precede first communion, but it became impossible everywhere for the bishop to make it to each parish all the time before children of seven received their first communion; so confirmation often was administered out of sequence after the children had already received the eucharist.

With the growing frequency of the postponement of confirmation to after first communion, the spirit of Jansenism resurfaced in pastoral practice and in religious education in the twentieth century. It was not eucharist, the sacrament that completes Christian initiation, but confirmation, the second sacrament, which was said to require lengthy catechesis, "mature" faith and other requirements of parish or catechetical policy before children or adolescents could demonstrate their worthiness to receive it.[3]

All the while, this custom of delaying confirmation was contrary to canon law; the 1917 code, canon 788, said that confirmation should be delayed to about the age of seven but that it could be given earlier if an infant were in danger of death or the minister had just and serious reasons for confirming soon. The contrary practice of delaying confirmation beyond seven only became an option in law in 1971, and this came about despite the views of liturgical experts who had recommended to Pope Paul VI that there be no change in the law.[4]

As a result of studies uncovering the history of confirmation, contemporary theologians have been critical of the above-mentioned "spiritual maturity" theology and praxis of confirmation. They argue not only that it does not correspond to the origins of the sacrament but also that it ritually and theologically demands too much of confirmation to the diminishment of baptism and eucharist. Baptism is the principal sacrament of faith in which believers receive the gift of the Holy Spirit. The other major sacrament of Christian life, the eucharist, is the sacrament that completes initiation into the church. When confirmation is delayed until after the reception of the eucharist, the sequence of initiation is disrupted, and it appears that confirmation, rather than eucharist, completes initiation. When greater maturity in the recipients is required for confirmation than for first communion, the significance of confirmation is maximized to the diminution of the eucharist. The appearance of a diminishment of baptism and eucharist in relation to confirmation also results from the practice of reserving confirmation for a higher-ranking minister, namely the bishop, than is typical for the celebration of baptism and first eucharist.

Canonical Discipline

The age prescribed in current canon law for the confirmation of those baptized as infants is "about the age of discretion," that is, about seven years of age, also called the age of reason (canon 891). The Rite of Confirmation, 11 states that confirmation is "postponed" until this age, which recalls the original practice of confirming immediately after baptism. If someone is in danger of death or when there is some other grave cause in the judgment of the minister, confirmation can be administered at another age, even to infants right after baptism. An "infant" in canon law is anyone under seven or anyone who lacks the use of reason.

Canon law does not require that those to be confirmed have the use of reason. The code says, rather, that "if they have the use of reason, they must be suitably instructed, properly disposed and able to renew their baptismal promises" (canon 889, §2). In the case of first communion, however, the use of reason is required, as well as "sufficient knowledge and careful preparation."[5] Thus, more knowledge and preparation are required in canon law of those receiving first communion than of those being confirmed.

A general exception to the age of seven is permitted for a region when its episcopal conference determines another age for confirmation as permitted by canon 891. According to this provision, it is possible that the age chosen by the bishops might be either earlier or later than seven. However, when canon 891 is read together with the Rite of Confirmation, 11, it is more likely that the legislator has in mind "a more mature age after appropriate formation."

Particular Law in North America

In 1985 the Canadian Conference of Catholic Bishops decreed that the sacrament of confirmation in the Latin rite shall be conferred at the age determined in the approved catechetical programs. The decree became effective in 1987 after it received the Holy See's *recognitio*, which is a kind of review necessary before a decree can be published. A commentary accompanying the published decree stated that "there is not necessarily one fixed age for confirmation in Canada. Rather, the age shall be determined in the approved catechetical programs of the country." It added that this "does not necessarily imply that an age higher than the one given in canon 891 must be chosen."[6] Thus, any age for confirmation is possible in Canada, provided it is stated in an approved catechetical program. Theoretically, this would not exclude confirming infants immediately after baptism if such a policy were to be permitted in an approved catechetical program.

In 1993 the National Conference of Catholic Bishops (NCCB) of the United States decreed "that the sacrament of confirmation in the Latin rite shall be conferred between the age of discretion, which is about the age of seven, and eighteen years of age, within the limits determined by the diocesan bishop and with regard for the legitimate exceptions given in canon 891, namely, when there is danger of death or, where in the judgment of the minister grave cause urges otherwise." This decree was approved by the Congregation for Bishops for a period of five years from July 1, 1994, through July 1, 1999.[7] According to the NCCB decree, the standard age for confirmation is between seven and eighteen. By exception, it can be administered to children below the age of seven in danger of death or when the minister of confirmation determines that there is another grave cause. In danger of death, any priest may validly and licitly confirm (canon 883, 3°).

The general rule in the United States is that the diocesan bishop determines the age within his diocese. This could be a single age or any age within the range of seven to eighteen years. However, the decree does not give the diocesan bishop the power to refuse the sacrament on the basis of insufficient age, provided the child is at least seven. Even though the practice of the diocese may be to have a higher age than seven as the usual time for confirmation, the diocesan bishop could not refuse to confirm a child of seven on the basis of age alone, since the age of seven is permissible both in universal law and the particular law of the episcopal conference. The bishop can determine certain limits, such as how often confirmation will be celebrated in a certain parish, who the ministers of confirmation will be, what the standard course of instruction will be, what the age usually will be and so forth. But these limits do not give him the authority to fix a minimum age different from that of the law of a higher authority.[8]

Children who have the use of reason have the same rights to the sacraments of confirmation, eucharist, penance and anointing of the sick that adults have. The fundamental canonical right to the sacraments is stated in canon 213 of the code. Canon 843, §1 states a corollary principle: "Sacred ministers cannot refuse the sacraments to those who ask for them at appropriate times, are properly disposed, and are not prohibited by law from receiving them." If the bishop is coming to a parish for confirmation, then that is most certainly an appropriate time to request the sacrament. All those seven and older would have the right to receive the sacrament at that time, provided they have been suitably instructed according to their capacity.

A baptized child of seven or older who has the use of reason and requests the sacrament of confirmation may and should receive it provided he or she is properly disposed, suitably instructed and able to renew the baptismal promises (canon 889, §2). A child who is judged to have the proper disposition and suitable instruction for first holy communion *de facto* has sufficient disposition and instruction to receive confirmation. The canonical requirement of "suitable" instruction in preparation for confirmation is relative to one's age and ability. The catechetical program for confirmation ought not be "set in stone," so absolute that a person who does not complete it cannot be confirmed. Catechesis must be geared to the level of the child, not to some general standard.[9] Besides, a child can always learn more about the sacrament after having received it. This is the ancient and venerable catechetical tradition called mystagogy.

For those baptized according to the RCIA, namely, those who are seven years or older and have the use of reason, all three sacraments of initiation *must* be given at the same celebration.[10] When those seven or older with the use of reason are baptized, their confirmation can be delayed only for a grave reason, for example, in danger of death when the minister who baptizes is not a priest or, even when he is a priest, if he lacks the sacred chrism. It is contrary to the law to postpone the confirmation of children who are of catechetical age when they are baptized simply because they have not reached the age of other confirmandi in the parish. This abuse also offends against good theology and deprives these children of a sacrament that they have a legal right to receive.

Given the wide range of ages for confirming in North America, it is important that each local church reflect seriously on the best age for the confirmation of children baptized as infants. Many theologians, canonists and pastoral ministers have devoted considerable study to the issue and have concluded on the basis of the history of confirmation, its ritual and theological relation to baptism and eucharist and the canonical discipline of the Latin church, that confirmation, when it legally cannot be administered immediately after baptism, ought then to be administered at the same celebration in which children of about seven make their first communion.[11] In liturgical law, this solution is most clearly seen in the Rite of Confirmation, 13, which states that Christian initiation "reaches its culmination in the communion of the body and blood of Christ. The newly confirmed *should therefore participate in the eucharist which completes their Christian initiation*" (emphasis added). This law says that the newly confirmed *should* make first communion in the same ceremony, not *must*. While it admits of exceptions, the law establishes what ought to be the normative practice.

The promotion of the cause of unity between the Catholic and Eastern churches is another important reason for returning to the original and proper sequence of sacramental initiation. The official Orthodox-Catholic dialogue commission, established by Pope John Paul II and Ecumenical Patriarch Dimitrios I, issued a statement that criticizes the practice "in certain Latin churches" of inverting the traditional order of the sacraments of initiation. The statement says: "This inversion, which provokes objections or understandable reservations both by Orthodox and Roman Catholics, calls for deep theological and pastoral reflection, because pastoral practice should never lose sight of the meaning of the early tradition and its doctrinal importance." The joint statement also notes that "the disciplinary directives which called for the traditional order of the sacraments of Christian initiation have never been abrogated."[12]

Minister of Confirmation

The original value behind the delay of confirmation seems to have been to allow the bishop, when he could not be present to baptize, at least to be able to perform the imposition of hands and anointing so that he could have some part in the initiation of each person in his diocese. This traditional value of the Western church can continue to be maintained by having the bishop come to parishes for confirmation when it is celebrated together with first communion. In this way, the proper sequence of initiation is maintained, the eucharist is seen as completing initiation, and the bishop's presence at confirmation, a lesser sacrament, does not appear to diminish the principal sacrament of the eucharist. Moreover, when the bishop presides at an important sacramental event in the life of the parish, it can be an effective reminder of his role as chief shepherd and principal liturgical celebrant in the whole local church.

In large dioceses where the bishop cannot celebrate all the confirmations, it seems fitting for him to delegate the pastor to confirm; the pastor has been entrusted with the pastoral care of the parish and is its recognized leader. Since the pastor typically presides at first communion, it follows that he also ought to preside at confirmation when it is celebrated with first eucharist and the diocesan bishop cannot be there. This is in keeping with canon 884, §1, which permits the diocesan bishop to give the faculty to confirm to a specified presbyter when need requires it. Demonstrating a case of need should include a consideration of: (1) the child's right, from age seven, to receive the sacrament; (2) the maintenance of the proper sacramental sequence; and (3) the importance of showing clearly the interrelationship between the sacraments of initiation and their culmination in full eucharistic participation.[13] Any one of these three reasons is serious enough for the diocesan bishop to delegate to a presbyter the faculty to confirm when he or another bishop is unable to celebrate it.[14]

Conclusion

Many experts on Christian initiation today, including those in the fields of theology and pastoral care, would welcome the restoration in the Western churches of the ancient practice of fully initiating all persons, even infants, with confirmation and eucharist following baptism.[15] Given the present canonical discipline of the Latin church, however, this is not possible at infant baptism. Therefore, the celebration of confirmation and first eucharist together at the age of about seven, which is the standard canonical age, is the best way of maintaining important theological and ritual values concerning confirmation's proper meaning and role within Christian initiation.

This is not simply the impossible dream of liturgists and canonists. It is becoming a reality in some dioceses and parishes in the United States, and it is likely to expand as more pastoral ministers and catechists become informed of the issues and are motivated to change. Practical proposals for restoring the proper sequence of the sacraments are available and can be implemented in a relatively brief period of time with proper planning, consultation and education.[16]

NOTES

[1] Some accessible liturgical studies on confirmation include Gerald Austin, *Anointing with the Spirit: The Rite of Confirmation; The Use of Oil and Chrism* (New York: Pueblo, 1985); Frank C. Quinn, "Confirmation Reconsidered: Rite and Meaning," *Worship* 59 (1985): 354–70; Aidan Kavanagh, "Confirmation: A Suggestion from Structure," *Worship* 58 (1984): 386–95; Gabriele Winkler, "Confirmation or Chrismation? A Study in Comparative Liturgy," *Worship* 58 (1984): 2–17; various authors in *Assembly* 14 (1987): 377–84; and *When Should We Confirm?* ed. James A. Wilde (Chicago: Liturgy Training Publications, 1989).

[2] Decree *Quam singulari,* August 8, 1910, AAS 2 (1910): 577–83.

[3] Linda Gaupin, "Now Confirmation Needs its Own *Quam Singulari*," in *When Should We Confirm?,* 85–93. On page 91 she comments: "Many of the practices formerly labeled abusive [by Pope Pius X] with the initiatory sacrament of eucharist still prevail today in our catechetical practices for confirmation."

[4] Annibale Bugnini, *The Reform of the Liturgy 1948–1975,* translated by Matthew J. O'Connell (Collegeville: Liturgical Press, 1990): 614.

[5] See canons 913–914. This general rule does not prohibit the administration of the eucharist to persons who are mentally retarded or who have other developmental disabilities. On this issue see my study, "Canonical Rights to the Sacraments," in *Developmental Disabilities and Sacramental Access: New Paradigms for Sacramental Encounters,* ed. Edward Foley (Collegeville: Liturgical Press, 1994): 94–115.

[6] *Studia Canonica* 21 (1987): 201.

[7] *BCL Newsletter* 30 (May 1994): 17.

[8] Canon 135, §2 states in part: "A law which is contrary to a higher law cannot be validly enacted by a lower level legislator."

[9] See the studies in *Issues in the Christian Initiation of Children: Catechesis and Liturgy* (Chicago: Liturgy Training Publications, 1989). In this work, pages 40–41, Aidan Kavanagh states that children "must be evangelized as they become capable, catechized so as to bring their nascent faith by appropriate stages to ecclesial term and (for those already baptized in infancy) initiated fully by confirmation and first holy communion in that order. . . . Programmatic, ideological or educational regimentation cannot obtain or direct the curious ways in which grace often works. It is to grace in the initiate that the church in its catechesis and sacraments must be appropriately obedient and faithful at whatever age." See "Historical Sketch and Contemporary Reflections," pages 33–43.

[10] See canon 885; RCIA, 208 (OICA, 34).

[11] Canonist Michael J. Balhoff reaches this conclusion in a thoroughly researched study based on his doctoral dissertation. See "Age for Confirmation: Canonical Evidence," *The Jurist* 45 (1985): 549–87.

[12] See Joint Commission for Theological Dialogue Between the Roman Catholic Church and the Orthodox Church, joint statement, *Faith, Sacraments and the Unity of the Church,* 51, August 1, 1987, *Origins* 17 (1988): 743–49.

[13] See Rite of Confirmation, 13; General Introduction to Christian Initiation, 2; canon 842, §2.

[14]Richard J. Barrett, "Confirmation: A Discipline Revisited," *The Jurist* 52 (1992): 697–714.

[15]See, for example, the studies from various disciplines in Mark Searle, ed., *Alternative Futures for Worship,* vol. 2: *Baptism and Confirmation* (Collegeville: Liturgical Press, 1987).

[16]See Frank D. Almade, "Age for Confirmation: A Proposal," *When Should We Confirm?,* 9–29.

Lay Preaching
at Liturgy

As the number of lay ministers who are qualified to preach increases, the issue of preaching by lay persons at liturgy becomes more important. The universal law of the Latin rite church governing lay preaching is given in canon 766: "Lay persons can be admitted to preach in a church or oratory if it is necessary in certain circumstances or if it is useful in particular cases according to the prescriptions of the conference of bishops and with due regard for canon 767, §1." Canon 767, §1 is on the homily: "Among the forms of preaching, the homily is preeminent; it is a part of the liturgy itself and is reserved to a priest or to a deacon; in the homily the mysteries of faith and the norms of Christian living are to be expounded from the sacred text throughout the course of the liturgical year."

Canon 766 says that lay persons can preach in accord with the policy of the episcopal conference; canon 767, §1 says they cannot preach the homily. These laws appear to be conflictual and have created much confusion. Even among canonists, the interpretation of the law is disputed. Moreover, in places like the United States where there is no uniform policy on lay preaching — despite efforts by the NCCB to enact one — greater uncertainty reigns about who may authorize it and under what circumstances.[1]

May lay persons preach at liturgy? May they preach at the eucharistic liturgy? If so, who may authorize it? What are the circumstances in which they may preach? These are some of the disputed questions whose answers lie in the proper interpretation of the law in text and in context, and in understanding the values that lie behind the law.

What Is a Homily?

The Pontifical Commission for the Authentic Interpretation of the Code of Canon Law issued an authentic interpretation on the issue of lay preaching. The commission was asked "whether the diocesan bishop can dispense from the norm of canon 767, §1, which reserves the homily to a priest or deacon." The answer was simply stated: "Negative."[2] As always, no reasons were given for the response. Canonists agree that the reason behind the decision is that the first paragraph of canon 767 is a constitutive law, and constitutive laws may not be dispensed (canon 86). A constitutive law defines the essential legal elements of an act or a thing. According to canon 767, §1, the homily contains four essential elements: (1) it is a form of preaching; (2) it is part of the liturgy itself; (3) it is reserved to a priest or a deacon; and (4) in the homily the mysteries of faith and the norms of Christian living are to be expounded from the sacred text throughout the course of the liturgical year.

The third essential element of this law indicates why the bishop may not allow a lay person to give a homily. A lay person cannot give a homily because by definition — by constitutive law — the homily is a form of preaching which can only be done by a priest or deacon and which can only be done at the liturgy. If a priest or deacon preaches outside the liturgy, he cannot give a homily because a homily by definition is liturgical preaching. Similarly, a lay person can never give a homily because by definition, a homily is a form of preaching which can only be done by a priest (presbyter or bishop) or deacon.

The legislator has defined the homily in a way that excludes its being preached by a lay person. This does not mean that a lay person can never preach. Canon 766 says that a lay person can be permitted to preach. Preaching is the genus; homily is one species of preaching. When a lay person preaches, it cannot be called a "homily" because that is impossible according to the way homily is defined in the law. It is akin to the president giving a presidential address. If anyone else gave it, it simply would not be a presidential address but some other kind of speech.[3]

What are the implications for lay preaching at the liturgy from this understanding of canon 767, §1 as constitutive law? Two outcomes are possible. The first possibility would be that the laity may never preach at liturgy under any circumstances, because a homily by a priest or deacon is the only form of preaching that can be given during the liturgy. The second alternative would be that a lay person could preach in certain circumstances during the liturgy, in accord with canon 766, precisely because they can never give the homily. Since, by definition, lay people cannot give a homily, then whenever they preach, whether it be during the liturgy or at some other time, it cannot be a homily. It is some other form of preaching.

What Is Liturgy?

If lay people cannot give a homily at liturgy, what does that mean? Does it mean every kind of liturgy, or only the eucharistic liturgy? One opinion is that "liturgy" means "eucharist." This opinion looks at paragraphs 2 and 3 of canon 767, which speak of the homily given during Mass.

> §2. Whenever a congregation is present, a homily is to be given at all Sunday Masses and at Masses celebrated on holy days of obligation; it cannot be omitted without a serious reason.

§3. If a sufficient number of people are present it is strongly recommended that a homily also be given at Masses celebrated during the week, especially during Advent or Lent or on the occasion of some feast day or time of mourning.

§4. It is the duty of the pastor or the rector of a church to see to it that these prescriptions are conscientiously observed.

The context established in paragraphs 2 and 3, according to this opinion, is seen to determine the meaning of liturgy in the first paragraph.[4]

However, if all four paragraphs of canon 767 were referring only to the eucharist, then this context should have been established in paragraph one. Instead, paragraph 1 defines the homily as preaching at liturgy by a priest or deacon. Paragraphs 2 and 3 then go on to speak of preaching at a certain kind of liturgy, namely, during the Mass. Paragraphs 2 and 3 do not alter the meaning of "liturgy" in paragraph 1 but give specific instructions for preaching at one kind of liturgy, the eucharist. The fourth paragraph does not mention anything about the eucharistic liturgy; it states that the pastor or the rector of the church is to see to it that these rules are conscientiously observed, and this can refer to preaching at eucharist or at another kind of liturgy.

If the legislator (the pope) had wanted to define the homily as that form of preaching done by a priest or deacon at the eucharist, he very well could have done so. But that is not the word the legislator chose. In canon 767, §1 the homily is defined as preaching at liturgy. The word "liturgy" is broader than the word "eucharist." The eucharist is only one form of the church's liturgy. Canon 834, §2 defines liturgy as worship carried out "in the name of the church by persons lawfully deputed and through acts approved by the authority of the church." These approved acts of the church are found in the liturgical books. They include all seven sacraments, the Liturgy of the Hours, all the sacramentals, funeral rites, eucharistic devotion outside Mass, the rite of religious profession, liturgies of the word, penance services and other approved forms of worship. It must be assumed that the legislator means what he says, that "liturgy" means "liturgy" and not "eucharist." To restrict the meaning of "liturgy" to "eucharist" may only be done by the legislator himself or by the Pontifical Council for the Authentic Interpretation of Legal Texts. The law means, therefore, that lay people may not give the homily at any liturgy, not just at the eucharist.

Lay Preaching in Liturgical Law

Can a lay person preach at liturgy? A lay person cannot preach the *homily,* because that is excluded in the law. This does not mean, however, that a lay person may never *preach* at the liturgy. The homily is only one form of preaching, that done by a priest or deacon at liturgy. Nevertheless, in a number of cases the law specifically allows a lay person to preach at a liturgy by using words other than homily. The laws in question are found in the liturgical books and in other liturgical documents.

The 1973 *Directory for Masses with Children* says that the pastor or rector of the church can permit an adult lay person to speak at a Mass for children after the gospel, especially if the priest finds it difficult to adapt himself to the mentality of children.[5] The 1988 *Directory for Sunday Celebrations in the Absence of a Presbyter* allows the lay leader at a celebration of the liturgy of the word or the Liturgy of the Hours to give an "explanation of the readings" after the scriptures of that liturgy have been proclaimed.[6] These provisions do not state that the lay presider can give a homily. The Holy See uses other expressions: "speaking after the gospel" in the one case, "an explanation of the readings" in the other.

The 1984 *Book of Blessings,* 21 allows lay catechists, lectors or other lay persons to be appointed to preside at various blessings. The blessings always include a liturgy of the word followed by an optional brief instruction on the readings, an exhortation or a homily. Three different terms are used here for the kinds of preaching that may follow upon the scripture reading: a brief instruction, exhortation or homily. There is no reason why the catechist, lector or other legitimately deputed lay presider at a blessing could not give an exhortation or a brief instruction on the scriptures, but he or she could not give the homily because that is restricted by law to a priest or deacon.

In the absence of a priest or deacon, and in accord with other provisions of the law, lay persons may also preside at liturgies of the word during the catechumenate, during eucharistic exposition, at funerals, at nonsacramental penance services and even at celebrations of baptism and marriage. All these liturgies, when presided over by a priest or deacon, usually include a homily after the readings. When a lay minister has been duly authorized to preside at such liturgies in the absence of a priest or deacon, there is no legal reason why the lay minister could not substitute some other form of preaching after the readings in place of the homily. This has been routinely done for many years by catechists and other lay leaders in mission countries. With the increasing role of lay presiders, this form of lay presiding and lay preaching will doubtless continue to expand. There is not yet a precise terminology for such lay preaching. The Holy See variously refers to it as speaking after the gospel, giving a reflection on the word, an exhortation or an instruction, or simply preaching. But it is not called a homily.

The distinction between a clerical homily and lay preaching is clearly enunciated in a statement of the Bishops' Committee on the Liturgy on Sunday liturgies without a priest:

> The preaching of a *homily* is part of most liturgical rites and is, by its very definition, reserved to a priest or deacon. However, the bishop may allow a lay person who is properly trained to explain the word of God at Sunday celebrations in the absence of a priest or deacon and at other specified occasions.[7]

According to the 1988 *Vatican Directory on Sunday Celebrations in the Absence of a Presbyter,* 43, lay presiders are also permitted to *read* a homily prepared by the pastor. Lay presiders cannot give the homily in their own words, since this is impossible by definition, but they may read a homily written by the pastor. In this latter case the homily is written by the ordained minister but is simply being read on his behalf by the lay presider. The homily remains the preserve of the ordained even if it is read by a lay person.

The only exception to this rule in the current liturgical books is found in the 1973 Rite of Infant Baptism, 26: "It is for the bishop to judge whether in his diocese catechists may give an improvised homily or speak only from a written text." This is an isolated exception which does not disprove the rule. Since the 1983 code came into force, which was reaffirmed by the authentic interpretation of canon 767, §1, it is no longer possible to speak of lay catechists or any other lay persons as giving homilies. This clarity of legal language did not yet exist in 1973. Now that the constitutive elements of the homily have been defined in the law, a subsequent edition of the Rite of Infant Baptism ought to find a substitute for the word "homily" when referring to some kind of lay preaching.

The evidence is abundant and conclusive that lay people may preach during the liturgy. The bulk of this evidence comes from officially approved liturgical books and documentation of the universal Latin-rite church. Lay people can preach at liturgy, but when they do so it cannot be called a homily unless they are reading a homily written by the pastor.

In all cases, liturgical presidency and preaching by a lay minister is an extraordinary ministry. An extraordinary ministry may be exercised in a case of need, that is, when the ordinary minister is absent or impeded. Canon 230, §3 states:

> When the necessity of the church warrants it and when ministers are lacking, lay persons, even if they are not lectors or acolytes, can also supply for certain of their offices, namely, to exercise the ministry of the word, to preside over liturgical prayers, to confer baptism, and to distribute holy communion in accord with the prescriptions of law.

All these extraordinary ministries may be permitted when the church needs them and when the ordained ministers are lacking or insufficient.

One of the ministries mentioned in canon 230, §3 is the ministry of the word, which, as canon 761 says, consists especially of preaching and catechetical formation. Thus lay persons may exercise the ministry of the word and preach at liturgy when the needs of the church require it and when ordinary ministers are lacking. Likewise, canon 766 says at first that lay persons can be admitted to preach in a church or oratory "if it is necessary in certain circumstances." However, the canon then goes further than the usual rule of necessity. It also allows preaching by lay persons in a church or oratory even when it is not strictly necessary, provided that it will be useful in a particular case in accord with the prescripts of the episcopal conference.

The Values Behind the Law

Up to now this analysis has centered on an interpretation of the words of the law, on their meaning in text and in context. However, this is not sufficient because it does not explain why the law is the way it is. A better interpretation of law must also ask what the values are that lie behind the law.

There are three key values at stake here. The first value behind the law is liturgical in nature. Preaching at liturgy is primarily a presidential role, that is, it is ordinarily and optimally a function of the presider. The one who presides over the liturgy of the word ought to be the one who preaches on the word of God. At Mass the priest presides over both the liturgy of the word and the liturgy of the eucharist, and he relates one to the other through the homily. The 1981 *Lectionary for Mass,* 24 describes this interrelationship:

> The purpose of the homily at Mass is that the spoken word of God and the liturgy of the eucharist may together become "a proclamation of God's wonderful works in the history of salvation, the mystery of Christ." Through the readings and homily Christ's paschal mystery is proclaimed; through the sacrifice of the Mass it becomes present. . . . Whether the homily explains the biblical word of God proclaimed in the readings or some other text of the liturgy, it must always lead the community of the faithful to celebrate the eucharist wholeheartedly. . . . From this living explanation, the word of God proclaimed in the readings and the church's celebration of the day's liturgy will have greater impact.[8]

The homily at Mass is ordinarily given by the presiding priest, as stated in the *General Instruction of the Roman Missal,* 42 and the *Lectionary for Mass,* 24. By exception the law permits another priest or deacon to give the homily. At Mass, the priest who presides over both the liturgy of the word and the liturgy of the eucharist ideally brings the two together through his homily, drawing out the riches of the word of God and leading the assembly's response to that word in praise, thanksgiving and communion. At a noneucharistic liturgy where a lay minister presides, the same principle holds: The lay minister optimally ought to be the one who preaches.

A second value of the law is to ensure that the preaching of God's word at liturgy is performed by qualified and competent persons. Those who preside at the church's liturgy must be

deputed for this function by their ordination, in the case of
the ordained, or by a commissioning or some other form
of deputation in the case of lay presiders. Because they are
acting in an official role in the name of the church, canon
law requires that such ministers receive adequate formation
(canons 231, §1; 232–264).

In the United States, seminarians preparing for the priesthood
typically have four or more years of theological and pastoral
studies, including courses in scripture, canon law, liturgy and
homiletics, and field education. Some schools of theology
and ministry in the United States are open to lay students. In
these institutions, lay people and religious are taking the same
courses as seminarians, and indeed some laity are getting
exactly the same degree as candidates for the priesthood — the
master of divinity. By virtue of their training, these lay men
and women are equally as qualified to preach the word of God
as the seminarians are. By contrast, the formation programs
for permanent deacons are far less substantial. Yet deacons, with
lesser formation, are allowed to preach a homily at liturgy and
at the eucharist when a priest presides.

Canon law presumes that the church's priests and deacons,
in virtue of their initial and ongoing formation, are qualified to
preach (canon 764). Obviously, canon law does not presume
that all lay people have professional formation for preaching.
However, when lay people have obtained a degree in theology or
ministry, or have had significant formal education in these areas,
then the third value behind the law will not be jeopardized by
permitting lay preaching at liturgy. The sacrament of holy orders
does not magically make a person an accomplished preacher.
That can only be achieved by study, prayer and hard work, whether
the preacher is ordained or lay.

The third value behind the law is the most fundamental. It
is, simply, that the word of God be preached to the people. Canon
213 speaks of the constitutional right of the faithful to receive
from their ordained leaders the word of God and the sacraments.
In order to ensure that this right is not neglected, the code insists
in various canons on the duty of the ordained ministers to see

that the word of God is proclaimed, preached and taught.[9] Preaching by the ordained is a duty; it is not a clerical privilege. The Second Vatican Council stated that preaching the gospel occupies an eminent place among the principal duties of bishops and that it is the first duty of presbyters.[10]

Although preaching is a primary and central duty of ordained ministry and is closely connected with it, it is not a power or orders. For bishops, preaching is a legal right, a right which allows them to preach everywhere; but it is also a right that can be restricted or denied in accord with the law (canon 763). For presbyters and deacons, preaching requires a faculty given in accord with the law. The law itself, in canon 764, gives to presbyters and deacons the faculty to preach everywhere under the conditions of that canon. The faculty does not come from holy orders but from the law, and the law places certain conditions on its being granted. The faculty is operative everywhere, but it can only be exercised with at least the presumed consent of the rector of the church, unless that faculty has been restricted or taken away by the competent ordinary or unless express permission is required by particular law.

The point of all this is to emphasize that preaching is not a power of orders, not a function that must be reserved to the ordained alone. Rather, it is a duty that pertains especially to the ordained. It is a duty imposed by the law so that the right of the faithful to the word of God will be ensured by its ordained ministers. As is stated in canon 766, however, there are times when this right of the faithful can also be promoted by lay preaching in churches and in oratories. These are in cases of necessity or usefulness. When it is necessary in certain circumstances or useful in particular cases, lay preaching, even at liturgy, can promote this fourth value of the law, the right of the faithful to be nourished by God's word.

Cases of Necessity and Usefulness

Is it lawful for a lay person to preach at the eucharist or at another liturgy when a priest or deacon is presiding? The answer is a qualified yes. Preaching by a lay person ought to be typical only at liturgies where a cleric is not presiding. Lay preaching at eucharist cannot be a routine occurrence without negating the principle that the one who presides normally ought to be the one who preaches.

However, exceptional situations can arise when the third value, the right to the word of God, would be promoted by preaching by a qualified lay person. The faithful have a right to hear the word of God proclaimed and preached, and the ordained ministers have the duty to preach it. There may be times when it is necessary for a lay person to preach or useful even if a priest or deacon is presiding at the liturgy. Necessity and usefulness — these are precisely the conditions for lay preaching required by canon 766. In a situation of necessity or usefulness, in accord with the prescripts of the episcopal conference, preaching by a lay person could be permitted even at a liturgy when a priest or deacon is presiding, although such preaching would not be the homily and must be called something else, such as an exhortation, an instruction, a reflection on the readings or the like.

The policy on lay preaching in Canada is a good example of what is meant by cases of necessity and usefulness. The Canadian policy permits lay preaching in these circumstances:

1) when there is no priest or deacon who can converse in the language of the people;

2) when the liturgy of the word is celebrated without a priest or deacon;

3) when seminarians who have begun their studies in theology are sent to parishes as part of their pastoral formation;

4) when certain circumstances require the participation of lay persons (financial questions, special appeals, special circumstances);

5) when the diocesan bishop judges it opportune.[11]

The first two are cases of necessity; the third and fourth are cases of usefulness; the fifth is a general category that might include either kind.

The cases of necessity and usefulness should be enumerated, at least in general fashion, in the policy of the episcopal conference. In the absence of a policy from the conference of bishops, the diocesan bishop is competent to develop norms for his diocese in keeping with his role as legislator for the local church; this includes the promulgation of laws and guidelines for the liturgy and preaching.[12] In the absence of a diocesan policy, one opinion holds that it falls to the pastor or other rector of a church to determine when a case of necessity or usefulness would recommend preaching by a qualified lay person.[13] While this opinion has merit, it would be more suitable to have a diocesan-wide policy that could ensure high standards for lay preachers and an enumeration of cases applicable to the situation of the local church.

Qualifications

Whoever preaches in a church or oratory should be qualified and competent. Lay persons, like clergy, should have appropriate formation if they are to preach in church. They should have sufficient knowledge in the fields of scripture and theology, and they should have preparation for or experience in public speaking. As noted above, lay religious and other lay persons are increasingly attending seminaries and graduate schools of theology and ministry, and they are taking the same courses and obtaining the same or similar degrees as those who are going to be ordained.

Not all lay persons who might be called upon to preach will have such clear-cut, certifiable competence. Sometimes a lay person may lack a formal degree but may be a good communicator, conversant with the scriptures and church teachings and committed to the gospel way of life. A diocesan policy should enunciate the formation and qualifications necessary for lay preaching by persons who lack a master of divinity or comparable graduate degree.

Ideally, the preparation of the laity and permanent deacons for the preaching apostolate should be no less exacting than that of priests. If the initial experience of the assembly is that lay preaching is mediocre or bad, preaching by lay persons will be resisted in the future, or people will go somewhere else where the preaching is better (as many already do when preaching by priests and deacons is poor). Lay preachers should strive to be equally as capable as their brothers in the clergy, if not better. Good preaching is welcome by the assembly; bad preaching is not. It is not enough for dioceses merely to enact a policy on lay preaching. Local churches must also see to it that lay preachers have the appropriate formation, even by granting financial assistance for the professional preparation of lay ministers.

NOTES

[1]On the various canonical viewpoints and on the NCCB's first policy that was not approved by the Holy See, see my talk to the Canon Law Society of America, published in CLSA *Proceedings of the 52nd Annual Convention* (Washington: CLSA, 1991): 61 – 79. The NCCB's second attempt to adopt a policy on lay preaching failed to get the necessary two-thirds vote of conference members.

[2]May 26, 1987, AAS 79 (1987): 1249.

[3]See William Skudlarek, "Lay Preaching and the Liturgy," Worship 58 (1984): 505.

[4]James Coriden proposes this opinion in "Teaching Office of the Church," in *The Code of Canon Law: A Text and Commentary,* ed. James A. Coriden, Thomas J. Green and Donald E. Heintschel (New York/Mahwah: Paulist, 1985): 553. However, he also recognizes that lay preaching is possible at the eucharist under certain circumstances.

[5]Congregation for Divine Worship, *Pueros baptizatos,* 24, November 1, 1973, AAS 66 (1974): 30 – 46; DOL 2157.

[6]Congregation for Divine Worship, *Christi Ecclesia,* 43, June 2, 1988, *Notitiae* 24 (1988): 366 – 78; *Origins* 18 (1989): 301 – 07.

[7]*Gathered in Steadfast Faith: Statement on Sunday Worship in the Absence of a Priest,* 55 f. (Washington: USCC, 1991). For a commentary see my article, "Sunday Liturgies Without a Priest," *Worship* 64 (1990): 451 – 60.

[8]Liturgy Documentary Series 1: *Lectionary for Mass Introduction* (Washington: USCC, 1982).

[9]See canons 386, §1; 528, §1; 756; 757; 762; 767, §§2, 3; 771.

[10]*Lumen gentium,* 25; *Presbyterorum ordinis,* 4.

[11]The decree was enacted in 1984 and was granted the *recognitio* of the Apostolic See in 1985. It is published in *Studia Canonica* 19 (1985): 174 – 77.

[12]See canons 386, 391, 756, 772, 835, and 838, §4. The archdioceses of Seattle and Milwaukee are examples of dioceses that have norms governing preaching by lay persons. The Seattle policy is quite good. A canonical weakness of the Milwaukee policy is that it does not determine cases of necessity and usefulness, nor does it even mention canon 766, where these two general criteria are stated as requisites for lay preaching.

[13]James H. Provost, "Brought Together by the Word of the Living God (Canons 762 – 772)," *Studia Canonica* 23 (1989): 363.

Acknowledgments

Translations of the canons are from *Code of Canon Law: Latin-English Edition,* copyright © 1983 by the Canon Law Society of America. Used with permission.

I am also grateful to the editors of the following copyrighted publications for permission to revise and update versions of my articles that appeared originally as follows:

Chapter 3: "The Sunday Mass Obligation, Past and Present," *Chicago Studies* 29 (1990): 262 – 276.

Chapter 4: "Daily Mass: Law and Spirituality," *Review for Religious* 50 (1991): 572 – 578.

Chapter 5: "The Liturgy of the Hours: Clerical Obligation, Prayer of the Whole Church," *Emmanuel* 97 (1991): 206 – 209; 224 – 225.

Chapter 6: "Penance, Canon Law, and Pastoral Practice," *Liturgical Ministry* 4 (1995): 31 – 36.

Chapter 7: "The Revised Code and Intercommunion," in *One Table, Many Laws: Essays on Catholic Eucharistic Practice* (Collegeville: The Liturgical Press, 1986): 85 – 97.

Chapter 9: "Options for Eucharistic Reservation" and "Eucharistic Reservation in Special Circumstances," *Federation of Diocesan Liturgical Commissions Newsletter* 17 (1990): 17– 20 and vol. 16 (1989): 29 – 32.

Chapter 11: "The Law on Lay Preaching: Interpretation and Implementation," *Canon Law Society of America Proceedings of the Fifty-Second Annual Convention* (Washington: CLSA, 1991): 61–79.

I wish to thank in a special way my mother, Rita T. Huels, for her help in word processing, and my editor at LTP, Martin Connell, PHD, for his trans-Atlantic assistance in getting this book into final shape.

John M. Huels

Index of Canons

1983 Code of Canon Law

canon	page
11	44
17	13
18	42
24	27
85	27
86	180
87	11
97, 2	49
107, 2	51
134	162
135, 2	11
204	26
208	27
213	40, 173, 187
216	26
226, 2	48, 51
230, 3	185
231, 1	187
232–264	187
246	79
246, 1	80
276	79
276, 2	92
381	11
391	11
392	11
608	161
609	161
663	79
678, 1	11
719	79
761	39, 185
763	188
764	187–188
766	179–181, 185, 188–189

767	181–182
767, 1	179–180, 182, 185
773	48
774, 2	48
776	48
777	50
793	48
834, 2	90, 182
835, 1	11
836	38–39, 43
837	16, 101, 163
838, 4	11
839, 2	11
840	38–40
841	17
842, 1	34
843, 1	41, 173
843, 2	43
844	115–116, 122–125, 147
844, 2	122–123
844, 3	116–123
844, 4	118–123
846, 1	10
851	44
868, 1	45–46
874	138–139
883	172
884, 1	47, 175–176
889, 2	47, 173
891	47, 171–172
904	79
907	16
913	49
913, 1	49
913, 2	49
914	49–50
915	51, 138
916	41, 51, 110
918	41–42

928	21
934	159
934, 2	162
935	164
936	159
937	163
938	155
938, 3	156
939	156, 162
944	11
960	51, 100, 109
961, 2	11, 104
962, 1	100, 110
964	106
964, 2	106
986, 1	105
988	51
988, 1	109
1041	144
1055	51, 146
1063	53 – 54
1064	54
1065, 2	53
1067	54
1077	54
1077, 1	54
1085	129
1099	53
1173	92
1174, 1	92
1174, 2	92
1175	94
1205	162
1210	162
1214	16, 162
1215	162
1216	20
1223	162
1224	162
1227	163
1247	68, 77

1248	68
1358	41
1752	14

1990 Code of Canons of the Eastern Churches

671	115–116, 125
671, 4	119
762	144
802	129
881	68
1240	138–139

1917 Code of Canon Law

135	75–76
595	75
731, 2	114
788	170
805	75–76
1081	146
1248	64
1249	64
1268	154
1367	75

Index of Liturgical Laws

citation   page

General Introduction to Christian Initiation
2   177

Rite of Christian Initiation of Adults
208   177

Rite of Baptism of Children
17   45
26   184–185
45   45

Rite of Confirmation
3   48
11   171
12   47–48, 58
13   47,
                                                                  174–176
23   48

General Instruction on the Roman Missal
2   173
21   22
42   186
276   155, 157
277   155–156

Lectionary for Mass
24   186

Rite of Holy Communion
and Worship of the Eucharist Outside Mass
5   160
9   155
10   155–156
13   156

Rite of Penance
4   97
5   101
7   107
13   105

18   101
19   101
22   101
37   102
40   112

Rite of Marriage
16   52

Book of Blessings
21   183

Rite of Dedication of an Altar
7   166

Liturgy of the Hours
10–17   91
11   94
13–16   90
15   91
19   95
29   92–94
33   88
77   94
108   92
242   89
246–252   88–89